For Every Dark Night... A Mother's Journey through Grief and Trauma

Diane Muller Ludman

iUniverse, Inc.
New York   Bloomington

iUniverse books may be ordered through booksellers or by contacting:
iUniverse

1663 Liberty Drive
Bloomington, IN 47403
www.iuniverse.com
1-800-Authors (1-800-288-4677)

ISBN: 978-1-4502-1572-5 (sc)
ISBN: 978-1-4502-1573-2 (ebook)

Printed in the United States of America

iUniverse rev. date: 03/29/2010

Dedication

This book is dedicated to my sons, the loves of my life.
Peter Jonathan Ludman
Michael Edward Ludman (in loving memory)

"Some people come into our lives and quickly go. Some stay for a while and leave footprints on our hearts. And we are never, ever the same."

Author Unknown

Table of Contents

Preface

This book is inspired by my desire to help others who are experiencing the loss of a child, for only those who have endured that horrific pain, numbing grief and indescribable trauma can connect with another. It is a life changing experience one can never imagine. It is beyond the imagination. The pain is devastating and unexplainable. Since I've always felt the need to deal with my feelings through writing, this book is my way of dealing with my pain, my grief and the shock of losing my twenty-two-year-old son Michael in an auto accident in August of 2002. I actually began writing a year later in the fall of 2003 when I "ran away" from home. I needed to get away from all my memories. Over the years I'd sit down to continue the chapters but would find myself in uncontrollable tears and would have to escape into that numbing place of denial for a while.

On the sixth anniversary of Mike's death in August of 2008 something very strange occurred. Arriving home from work, I discovered a message on my answering machine from a woman who thought she had called the cemetery. She was very distraught and emotional. She explained that someone was disturbing her son's grave. The next message was an apology for the call; she had dialed the wrong number. But I knew the message was no coincidence. I returned her call immediately and we talked for over thirty minutes. The woman was very raw since it had only been a few months since her son's death. He was about the same age as Mike when he also died in a tragic accident. Eventually this distraught mother asked me if I had observed any strange occurrences since the death of my son. Our conversation became very interesting at that point. Only one bereaved parent to another can talk about such things without the threat of judgment. For me, this was a sign from Mike that I needed to continue to help other grieving parents and to reach out to touch the hearts of those suffering through their own pain, grief and trauma.

Shortly after that phone call, I attended a seminar with Shawn Doyle, a well-known motivational speaker, courtesy of my employer. Through the work I did in that workshop, and with the encouragement from my small group and Shawn, I knew I had to return to my story. As a courtesy, he asked to read several of my chapters, which I sent to him via e-mail. His response was very inspiring as he persuaded me to continue my writing and to find a publisher. As you will discover, I believe there are no accidents. Things happen at the right time for a reason.

There is one thing I need to explain before continuing. You will find my son's name spelled many different ways. I refer to my son Michael as Mike, Mikie or Lovebug. His older brother Pete and many friends spelled his name Mikey, so you will see his name spelled differently in different contexts. Most of Mike's friends lovingly refer to him as Big Worm or Worm. They all had nicknames.

It is my hope that the bereaved will find some comfort and solace in my stories. All the experiences are real and there are many more I could share, but I could bare my soul only so much. It is still difficult to sit down and spend a day with Mike through my writing. As I continued to write, more memories surfaced, but those are memories that are with me every day and too many to include here, for I know they will never end.

There are so many people to thank for their love and support over these last years. They know who they are. I choose not to name them all in fear I will omit someone dear. As I said, there were those who stood by me, supported me and looked after Mike's brother Pete and me. Mike's friends still include me in their lives and special occasions. I am grateful to all of you.

A special thanks and acknowledgement goes to Lisa Roark for her permission to enhance my story with her beautiful, poignant poetry. Lisa attended KinderMourn, a support group for bereaved parents, during my eighteen months there. Eventually she began to open and close each session with her poems. Her words were so meaningful; it was as if any one of us could have written those heartfelt words. I would also like to acknowledge and thank my devoted friend, and editor, Joanna Sheldon for her expertise and for the countless hours she spent editing my stories. She was relentless. My gratitude and appreciation to Cindy Gaines Nims – she contributed her time and talent to create the exceptional and inspired cover in Mike's honor. My undying gratitude and love goes to my son, Peter, for his ongoing support for his mom and for his continuous technical and graphic support. They were all indispensable in bringing my story to fruition.

To those reading this book, I wish you comfort, peace, healing and love.

Diane Muller Ludman

Our Last Snow Day Together

It was unusual that January of 2002 to have both my boys home in the weeks after Christmas. Pete was twenty-three and lived in Knoxville, Tennessee, where he graduated from The University of Tennessee in Architecture. He remained there working with an architectural firm to achieve his dream of becoming an architect. Mike was twenty-one and lived with friends in Wilmington, North Carolina, where he was employed as a plumber's apprentice. He enjoyed being outdoors and working with his hands, as he continued to obtain the required hours to become a licensed plumber. He and Pete often talked about how they would refer jobs to each other.

It was a cold, bleak day and we resigned ourselves to staying in and hanging out at home. Pete wasn't feeling well; he had suffered a bad allergy attack from being around his Dad's cat a few days earlier. By late morning it started to snow, a hard snow with perfect snowman-making white powder. That got Mike's attention. The day changed from dreary to exciting. Mike and I found our ski outfits and decided to head out to play in the snow and build a snowman. Then the phone rang. It was one of Mike's friends offering to come out to pick him up from BFE (a slang expression Mike often used to describe our new home in the suburbs). His friends wanted him to have a play day with them. I felt an instant disappointment until I heard Mike say, "No, man, I'm staying home and building a snowman with my Momma." The fun memories of previous snow days when the boys were young came to mind. My grown son actually wanted to stay home with his mom and his big brother. "What a beautiful, beautiful gift!" I thought to myself. There's nothing sweeter to a mom.

As we donned our snow attire we prodded Pete to come out and play in the snow. He fought it for a while, then grabbed the camera to take pictures of us having a sword fight with icicles we pulled from the eaves of the house and throwing snowballs at each other. We laughed and giggled while ducking from the path of the hard packed snowballs. Finally, Pete could no longer resist when Mike attacked him with snowballs as he peeked out the patio door with the camera. He joined in the fun, even with his runny nose and miserable stuffy head.

Now it was time to build a snowman. Pete was our snowman architect. He was always thinking outside of the box, so this would be no ordinary snowman. Our snowman was going to be "unplugged and seated!" We grabbed one of the patio chairs and began rolling the cold, hard snow while still ducking incoming snowballs.

Children will be children, and we were all children that day. We played together laughing and smiling. We hadn't done anything like this in a very long time. I remember thinking, "Hold this moment in your heart, because you never know if you will have another occasion like this." Spontaneous moments of pure childlike joy had been few and far between since the boys grew up and started their own lives.

As Mike and I began placing the rolled balls of snow on the patio chair, Pete grabbed a butter knife from the kitchen and began to etch out the details of the snowman. Pete was the detail man. Always was. I'll never forget the laughter and fun we had that day – just the three of us. Thank God I recognized the gift as it was happening and I soaked up every ounce of pure enjoyment surrounding us. Pete and Mike were always close growing up and still had a very strong bond between them. Pete always looked out for his little brother. Once, when they were very young, I found him teaching Mike the alphabet, and when he discovered me peeking through the door, he glanced up and told me I could watch but I couldn't help.

Pete created the snowman or "snow dude," as we referred to it, seated in the patio chair with its elbows relaxed on the chair arms. When it was almost finished, I grabbed a white Panama hat and sunglasses for the accessories. We found candy and fruit for the eyes and mouth and, of course, we had to insert a piece of straw in its mouth to make the picture complete. Being so caught up in the gaiety of the adventure, I ran into the house and found an almost empty Grand Marnier bottle, which I nestled in its hand, so it appeared as if he was drinking from the bottle. Mike took the seat next to it and pretended the snow dude was giving him a drink. It was quite a work of art, and we did it together with so much fun, so much laughter, and so much love. That's what our day was made of - love.

When our neighbors came out to play in the snow, we teamed up to have another snowball fight. This time we were all on the same side. Then the boys helped the little three-year-old and her mom and dad build their own snowman. This one was a very traditional snowman.

What a day! We were so cold and frost bitten that we finally surrendered and went inside to defrost. Then a thought hit me. What a great opportunity for *Tea Time*. Since the boys were young, we would set aside some quality time we called *Tea Time*. The television would go off and we would sit at the table with a pot of hot tea and cookies or crackers and talk. We talked about anything and everything – our day, school, friends, wishes, and sometimes even feelings. Ninety-nine percent of the time the boys would choose *Tea Time* over a favorite television program. We hadn't had that special occasion together in many years. When I suggested *Tea Time*, it was unanimous. I put the water on to boil.

The sky started to darken as the afternoon waned. We gathered around the kitchen table for some hot tea, crackers and conversation as we laughed and reminisced about our day in the snow. Again, I thought, "Hold this moment in your heart, for you never know when it will happen again." I knew I had been given a truly wonderful gift. Although at the time, I thought there would be more – maybe not soon, but sometime.

How precious time is, how truly precious. Now I fully understand what an incredible gift I was given that day –

a day of love and joy and togetherness that would never happen again. I was given a treasured memory, which no one can ever take away from me. Today I embrace it tightly in my heart, our last snow day together.

A Fragile Beginning

The first time I saw my son, after his birth, he was flat on his back in an incubator with an IV in his arm, gasping for the oxygen his little body so desperately needed to survive. He spent the first seven days of his life on life support. Two gauze pads covered his beautiful brown eyes to protect them from the bright bililight that surrounded him to prevent jaundice. Michael entered this world five weeks before we expected him. I believe he was anxious to do what was his to do. Throughout his life he was known to be a little impatient and I guess this is where it all began.

While other mothers had their babies brought to them, I paced the hospital halls alone, and anxiety overwhelmed me as I worried if my son would survive. I sat patiently in the preemie ward waiting for any chance to touch my precious child, to hold him and rock him and love him.

When he was six days old, his dad and I were told he needed a blood transfusion because of his increased, and possibly dangerous, jaundice level. My fear for his survival elevated. But then hope returned when we were told the next day that his jaundice had decreased to an acceptable level. He wouldn't need a blood transfusion, and we could take him home. Looking back, I believe that on some other level of consciousness he was still deciding whether or not he wanted to stay in this world. What a blessing he decided to stay.

He was born Nathan Edward Ludman, my tiny little Nate. However, when it was time to take our son home from the hospital, his dad confessed he really didn't like the name Nathan, so we changed his name to Michael Edward - my Mikie.

It's so strange the way life plays out. My darling son came into this world hooked up to life support, with gauze-bandaged eyes, and he left it the same way twenty-two years later. He left us much too early – again teetering for a short time between life and death. Once again, I sat at his side holding him and loving him as his body gasped for air. Again he laid on his back on life support. One look into his beautiful brown eye on that August night told my heart he was gone. And this time it would be forever. I would never see his wonderful smile again.

The pain was unbearable, unimaginable. His leaving left a hole in my heart and the hearts of so many of his family and friends that left us wounded and racked with grief.

My Darkest Night

The night was Friday, August 16, 2002. I received *the phone call* – the most dreaded phone call, the one all parents fear. "Hello, is this Ms. Ludman, the mother of Mike Ludman?" A rush of panic swept over me as my heart ached at those ominous words.

Mike was on his way to Wilmington, the place he loved and had lived for most of the past year, to visit friends and to celebrate the twenty-second birthday of his closest friend, Adam, also known as his "other brother." Adam was already in Wilmington when Mike called to say that he and their friends, Nick and Serena, were on their way. It was raining, the first rain we had received in so very long, which made the winding, narrow one-lane highway slick and dangerous.

What is it about our sixth sense that we don't acknowledge? Adam wanted them to wait because the weather was too bad. Later I was told that he paced the floor after the call, feeling that something wasn't right. But, these were twenty-something-year-olds. It was Friday night and they were on their way to the beach, on their way to a party to be with their "family of friends." Some were already there, others were to follow the next morning.

I worked late that Friday to finish a project document. Mike called me when he arrived home from work to tell me Nick was picking him up in a few minutes and they would wait at Chris' house, the hangout house, for Serena. Once she got off work, they would be on their way. I told him I loved him, to have fun and be careful and I would see him Sunday night.

Little did I know I would see him that very, gut-wrenching night. I would see Mike in a way no mother should ever see her child. I would see him in bandages still caked with blood. I would see him on oxygen gasping to breathe. I knew, the moment I saw him, he was gone. Yet I prayed for a miracle. I held on for a miracle all through the night, but it was not to be.

The man on the other end of the phone nervously apologized for calling me with the news, of which he knew very little. All he could tell me was that he lived on Highway 218. He was in his yard when two ladies stopped and urged him to call me to inform me my son had been in an accident. He didn't have any details, only that there was an accident and cell phones were not working. No 911 calls were ever made. The two women had seen paramedics at another accident and insisted they rush to the site of Mike's accident. The only information he gave me were the phone numbers for the Anson County and Union County hospitals and police stations, since he wasn't sure in which county the accident had occurred.

"This can't be happening!" I cried. If Mike were able, he would call me himself. Why was I hearing the news from a stranger? Mike had been involved, as a passenger, in two accidents in the last six months, and I didn't even know about them until after the fact. He was never the driver, always a passenger. This time I knew it was bad. My stomach was churning. I wanted to go searching the highway for Mike, but friends urged me to wait until I heard something more definite. For nearly an hour, I called the police stations and hospitals. "No, no one was brought in by that name" or "No, we don't have an accident report in that area." Then, I heard the words I will never forget. "Yes, your son was just brought into the emergency room," the ER nurse at Union Memorial Hospital reported, "but don't come here. We're transporting him to Carolinas Medical Center in Charlotte." They were taking Mike to the trauma center. All she could tell me was that Mike had severe injuries. My legs gave out. Tears of fear began flowing. "We're taking him to Carolinas Medical Center" were words of doom.

I knew it was bad; it was really bad. I called his father, Ed. I could hear his fearful tears and distress as he hurriedly agreed to meet me at the hospital and ended the call. Hearing Ed's response reinforced my own fears. I then called a friend to take me to the hospital. I don't know why, for some strange sense of comfort maybe, but I grabbed the first rosary I could find. I also took the angel on Mike's night table – a duplicate of the one he had placed in his grandfather's coffin two and a half years earlier – one to be with his grandfather and one to be with

Mike forever. It sat on his night table with a Bible, a gold cross and his grandfather's softball, which was very special to Mike. He and his grandfather both played baseball and both excelled at the sport. They, too, shared a special bond. It suddenly occurred to me that Mike had taken the baseball, the angel and the Bible with him to our family reunion in Pensacola the weekend before. He had never taken those items with him on a trip ever before.

On the long, terrifying ride to the hospital, I pleaded with the Blessed Mother. I knew she could understand. She had watched her son die, and I pleaded with her not to let that happen to my Mikie. Later I discovered from his brother, Pete, that the rosary was Mike's First Communion rosary. I had it with me all through the night and thought it belonged to Pete.

Then the nightmare worsened – the horror, the disbelief, the eerie fog. As I entered the emergency room, I saw Mike's dad, and then I saw four of Mike's best buddies – Josh, Nelson, Trevor and Sean. They were sitting at the far end of the waiting room, their heads hung low in a stunned silence. I knew they knew something I didn't yet know. It was hard for them to make eye contact. They each hugged me, then went back into their eerie silence – waiting. My dear friend Helen and her daughter Lynn arrived. Helen was always so supportive and had a very spiritual presence. I believed her to be the "Wise Woman." Helen was my mentor, my spiritual advisor and my trusted friend. She came to mean a lot to the boys and me. Mike once referred to her as "a frigging wonderful woman" and he meant it from his heart.

We waited. We saw the ambulance arrive, but still they made us wait. Finally, a doctor appeared. He was very professional and direct, no softening the blow. "Your son suffered severe head trauma and brain damage." Did I really hear those words? That was not what I thought we would hear. I expected to sit with Mike for as long as it took for him to recover. How could that doctor stand there and tell his parents such a horrific statement – a death sentence before he was pronounced dead. It was unacceptable! It was unforgivable! It was a lie! It had to be a mistake!

The doctor led us through sliding glass doors to the emergency entrance to see Mike before they took him for tests to confirm the severity of his injuries. It was only a formality. They already knew. It only took one look to know the unbelievable was true. My son, my beautiful, loving son, his head and neck and left eye caked in bloody bandages and his right eye half open, staring off into another world as his chest heaved heavily to breathe. I kissed his sweet face, hugged him and told him it would be okay. "I love you Mikie," I whispered, as they rolled the gurney down the hall away from us. They should let us stay with him. He needed to know we were with him. I watched him go and fell to the floor wailing, clutching his angel, knowing he was gone. Then I remember his dad lifting me from the floor and telling me I couldn't do that. Why? What did it all matter? What did anything matter?

Someone led us to a small family room where we both sat in bewilderment. Now it was Ed's turn to cry uncontrollably as he held onto me. Was this reality or a horrible dream? It felt like a dream, unreal, yet scary and vague. My body didn't know how to move, my brain didn't know how to function, my lungs didn't know how to breathe, my heart didn't know how to stay in my chest. I wanted to wake up, I wanted a do-over – I wanted this all to go away.

It was all so strange. We were escorted to a larger room closer to Mikie. One by one, more of Mike's friends filled the room, which was engulfed in an eerie silence. When Nick and Serena arrived, I realized they hadn't been there before, and I had no idea what had happened to them. I saw Nick's shirt covered in blood. I remember asking him whose blood was on his shirt. He said it was his. I nodded silently, knowing it wasn't. The blood was right where Nick would have held Mike's head in his arms. I don't know why I asked such a question about something I already knew the answer. I guess I wanted to know more, but it wasn't the time or the place. What was happening was more than I could comprehend. I only recall scenes, instances from that long journey through the night.

At some point, we were told that there was no hope. It was only a matter of time before Mike's brain stem would die. Still more of Mike's friends filled the room. They were his "family of friends" who were so important to him. I don't remember telling them Mike wasn't going to make it, but I do remember realizing all those friends were here to see Mike, and they should be able to do so. Mike would have wanted each of them to be able to say good-bye in their own way.

When the nurses agreed to let them in to see Mike, two at a time, I fell deeper into the dark abyss. I knew that wasn't allowed at two or three, or whatever time it was, in the middle of the night. The nurses knew Mike's friends were really saying their final good-byes.

By this time two more of my dearest friends, Joanna and Tracey, had arrived and were holding vigil and praying together in another small family room. I am still amazed to this day that Tracey found her way to the hospital so late at night. Because of problems with her eyesight, she never drove after dark and often had trouble with directions. But somehow she made her way to me to offer support and join in the prayers for Mike. They held me as I lay exhausted on a sofa while I left Mike's side so all his friends could be with him. What a strange sight, to see all those devoted friends waiting in the hallway to have their turn to say a final farewell to their buddy.

Then I saw my son Pete. Thank God Ed had called him as soon as he ended the call with me. Pete was living and working in Tennessee. If Ed had not called when he did, Pete would have missed being with Mike throughout his last night. He was on his way out the door to celebrate a new project he had been given at his architectural firm. Instead, he grabbed his bag, still full of beach attire from our family reunion in Pensacola the weekend before – the last time he saw Mike and said, "See you later, Man" as Mikie and I headed for the airport. Pete rushed to Charlotte, a four-hour drive over the mountains in pouring rain, trying to make it in time to give Mike a kidney or blood or whatever he needed. Pete had always watched over Mike and now he believed he would be the one to save his brother's life.

When I saw the pain and anger on Pete's face I realized someone had already told him the truth. I ran behind him, trying to stop him, to explain how he was going to see his brother, but he was unstoppable. I had never seen my son like this before. He was only focused on Mike, and fighting the fear of what he was told before he even saw Mike. I caught up to him as he reached the foot of Mikie's hospital bed, just as he fell to the floor engulfed in pain, grief and disbelief. I dropped beside him, took him in my arms, held him, rocked him and let him sob – that deep sob from his gut, wails of unimaginable pain and disbelief. Mike's friends fled the room to give us our privacy.

As our vigil with Mike continued the nurses tried to offer comfort. They were like sweet angels. They brought us blankets to cover the cold, orange plastic chairs – anything to try to make our last moments together more comfortable. There really wasn't much else they could do. Pete, Ed and I took turns sitting in the chair on Mikie's good side – the side of his face that wasn't bandaged, the side we could kiss and wipe with a cool washcloth as we whispered in his ear. We talked to him all through the night and hugged him and kissed him. Friends took turns guiding me to the bathroom to ease my sick stomach. Ed went outside to smoke cigarettes. Pete mostly stayed by Mike's side, but took occasional smoke breaks with his dad. Pete is such a blessing – he was always there for all of us – Mike, Ed and me. We each had our own personal and private moments with our Mikie. We each had different relationships with Mike and we all loved Mike dearly and unconditionally.

It's funny the things you remember. I recall telling Pete to rub Mike's feet as I sat next to him, kissing his face, holding his hand, rubbing his arm and talking to him. I wanted to make sure Mike could feel us touching him and know we were with him. The nurses told us Mike had no neurological responses, there was no hope and we needed to take him off of life support. The nurses tried often to convince us to let Mike go. They described in detail what the end would be like when Mike's brain stem died. But I wouldn't give up hope for my miracle. He had beaten the odds before, and I wasn't giving up now.

A priest was called in by the hospital minister to give Mike the Last Rites. Although I was no longer a practicing Catholic, we all were raised in the Catholic Church and the sacrament of the Last Rites felt like the right thing to do. It really hadn't occurred to me until the priest arrived, because I was focused on Mike's survival, not his death. I believe I really knew the truth in my heart and allowed the ceremony. However, I still denied the unacceptable.

A surge of hope returned when a tear fell from Mike's eye. A few minutes later, another tear appeared on his bloody cheek. I called for the nurses. Surely, they were mistaken – Mike did have a chance for a miracle. Even Ed believed. He and Mike had a disagreement that hadn't been settled and after seeing the tears shimmer down Mike's cheek, Ed asked to have some time alone with him.

As the night wore on and the Kleenex piled up on the floor, Mike would have spells of labored breathing – his whole body seemed to be in distress. The nurses would come to his side to inject morphine into his IV tube and Mike would settle down. Hope. It gave me hope. I would have my miracle. Through swollen eyes I repeatedly told the nurses and doctor they were wrong. Mike was responding, he was feeling something. After several episodes, Pete finally looked me in the eye with a sad, compassionate expression and said, "Mom, they're not giving Mike the morphine for him, they're giving it to him for you – it relaxes his muscles. They're only doing it for you, Mom." The truth is so brutal! Then Pete added, "That's not Mike, he's right here on the side of the bed with us." My God! My son was giving back to me all the things I taught him and knew to be true, but it was disturbing when it directly applied to me. I knew Pete was right. Or was it Mikie, letting Pete know? They were always so close and I'm sure Pete picked up on Mike's thoughts. Even when they were very young, before I could understand what Mike was saying, Pete would translate for him. They had a strong, brotherly bond – something special between them that only they could understand. Mike's first words were, "Bi Bro," for big brother, and Mike referred devotedly to Pete as "my brother" for the rest of his life.

As daylight peeked through the window, I realized it was time to call my family in New Orleans. I was still hoping for my miracle and could not truly accept what I knew to be true from the first moment I saw Mike on the ambulance gurney. But Ed had been in contact with his side of the family throughout the night, and I didn't want my family to hear about Mike's accident from someone else. Helen had the nurses arrange a long distance call for me. I don't know who I was when I made that call. I was detached. I wasn't the person my family knew me to be. I remember Helen taking the phone from me and talking with my mother. She must have relayed the truth that I could not accept. It was strange. I let go of the concerns of what my family would do once they heard the news. Would they come to Charlotte immediately? How would they handle the horrific news of our Mikie? I couldn't think about that now.

The doctor and nurses had been relentless in explaining Mike's prognosis and in urging us to let him go – to give Mike permission to go. One of the nurses held me in her arms and whispered in my ear, "Honey, it's time to let Mike go."

"No! No! No!" I looked at her and sighed, "It's not okay to let him go." I was running out of hope. Where was my miracle? Just then Megan and her mom walked through the door.

Megan! I had forgotten about Megan – Mike's love of his life. They were experiencing some problems in their relationship at the time. Unfortunately, she hadn't heard about Mike's accident until she had a message on her machine in the morning. She had no idea of what had happened the night before. Megan didn't expect Mike to be on his deathbed when she arrived by his side. We gave them some time alone. Megan needed her special time with Mike – they had been together since their junior year in high school. Now I look back and believe Mike was waiting for Megan before he could leave.

Once Megan arrived, his condition continued to deteriorate. I sat again holding Mike and kissing his cheek. We were all gathered around his bed when we heard the horrible, awful, hope-ending sound of water flowing into a pail. "What's that sound?" I asked numbly. But I knew before Pete glanced at me so mournfully, so knowingly. "Mom?" was all he said. It was the sound of Mike's kidneys failing – the sound of the end. As his body heaved, gasping for breath, I knew it was over. Our vigil had ended. Mike was leaving us and we had no control over his life – it was now in God's hands. In my heart I knew he had not been in his physical body from the moment he was thrown so forcibly from the car. He was, as Pete had said, sitting on the side of the bed with us, holding us as we held him.

In a trancelike state, we signed papers to have Mike's eyes donated to someone who needed them. What a gift, to have someone else be able to see through those beautiful, brown eyes. Helpless, we watched as the nurses turned off the life support machine. "Come on, Mike," I kept whispering in his ear, "Show them they were wrong. You can do it, Lovebug. I always told you that you could do anything you wanted to do, you could be anything you wanted to be if you wanted it bad enough. Fight, Mikie, fight!"

Maybe he had seen the white light and knew that's where he would find peace. Maybe he knew this was his time. Somehow, on another level, I think we all know when it's our time to go. Mike left us a little before noon on Saturday. They let me stay with him for what seemed too short a time, but it was maybe an hour or two, holding him, touching him, kissing him. My son, my child, my beautiful Mikie. How could I let him go? Why did they make me finally leave? How could I go on never to be with Mike again, never to touch his face, never to see his smile, never to feel his hugs, never to hear his laugh? His pain was over. Mine was just beginning.

Reflections

Now I look back and realize how strange that Friday afternoon was for me. As I walked to my car, about six-thirty that evening, I thought to myself, "It's time to write a story for Mike to let him know how proud I am of him." When Pete graduated from college, I wrote a story about his leaving home and knowing things would never be the same. I wanted to let him know how proud I was of him. That story, *The Suitcase,* stayed between Pete and me. It was personal. So, too, would be my story for Mike. I wanted to let him know I admired him for working so hard at a profession he truly enjoyed, for persevering despite all the obstacles he faced and how I could see the changes in him as he moved forward.

Since Mike returned home from Wilmington at the end of May, he had settled into a routine. He got up early, made himself breakfast, and waited for his ride to work.

Sometimes he wouldn't get home until seven or seven-thirty in the evening. I was so amazed at how he worked all day in the heat, yet he always managed to walk in the door with a smile. Mike told me not to worry about him, "I'm young," he would boast. "I can take it."

Later, at Mike's wake, I felt so blessed to hear from a coworker of his that Mike was always smiling and laughing on the job. He loved what he did, and he did it well. Both my boys had such a strong work ethic. I was in awe of them both. I was, and still am, so proud to be their mother. Being their mother was my favorite thing in this life.

In the evening, when Mike came home, we would watch *Jeopardy*, at my coaxing, followed by *King of the Hill*. Jeopardy was not really Mike's thing, but we did it together, then after dinner the TV was his. We had dinner each evening, except on weekends – that was the time for his friends. Since we moved away from the old neighborhood, to BFE, and Mike was not driving, he depended on friends to pick him up to go out and party. Usually, he spent the night at a friend's house on Fridays and returned home exhausted on Saturday afternoons. In those last two and a half months of his life, Mike was more content than I had ever seen him.

I remember when we went shopping together to look for tennis shoes. That was no small task for Mike. It had to be the right shoes. He was a very choosy dresser, as most of his friends can attest. They told me they spent many an evening waiting for Mike. He was always checking out how he looked. His Nautica shirt had to match his shoes, and he was never quite sure if his outfit was exactly the way he wanted. He was always changing his mind and

21

making his friends wait. Yet he'd walk out twenty minutes later and look exactly the same. His friends' words still echo in my ears from high school days when I asked what they were doing sitting on my front steps as I returned home. "What do you think we're doing Ms. Ludman? We're waiting for Mike!" In the years since Mike's death, I've come to understand that was pretty much the way things went.

Mike and I spent more quality time together than we had before he moved out on his own. We went to the movies a few times after he returned home – something we hadn't done since he and Pete were younger. I would buy the tickets and he would buy the popcorn. Strangely, the last movie we saw together was about a minister who lost his faith after his wife died in bizarre car accident. His child's life was later saved because of a message from his deceased wife. The movie was *Signs*. Now I look back and realize that was no accident. It was in itself a sign, a sign of things to come.

That Painful Day

The things of this life that seemed so important,
Have lost the meaning they had before,
Since he stopped to say I love you,
And he turned and walked out of the door.

So many things I would have told him,
On that awful painful day,
If somehow I could have known,
I would never have the chance to say.

I would have told him how much I loved him,
And I would have begged him not to go,
I would have held him in my arms,
My love for him to show.

I would have told him that no matter what,
He had ever said or he had ever done,
That I was always so proud of him,
And I was so glad he was my son.

I would have let him know the blessed joy,
That it was to watch him grow,
To become that handsome man,
That everyone should have had the chance to know.

But Heaven needed another angel,
So God just let him walk away,
Into His arms for Him to hold him,
On that awful painful day.

By Lisa Roark
A KinderMourn Mom
Mother of Darryl Roark, Jr.

The Funeral

Leaving the hospital Saturday afternoon, I was in a state of shock and disbelief. Helen was still by my side and took Pete and me home after spending the entire night with us throughout our hospital vigil. I don't know how she had the energy to take care of us and organize everything. She assured me, "I'm not leaving you," and she never did, even though she was suffering with her own grief.

As I sat like a zombie in my living room chair, I asked Pete to get Mike's towels and washcloths he had used before his trip and told him to close Mike's bedroom door. I don't know why, but at the time it was very important to me, as if I could hold onto Mike in some way. Meanwhile, my friends – Kathy, Alice, Dagmar and June had arrived and Helen had contacted my physician to have him prescribe medication to sedate me. The last image I have of that surreal and horrific day was lying in bed with my friends holding on to me and consoling me, while trying to hold back their own tears.

When I awoke in a disoriented daze Sunday morning, my sister Mary Lee was there, patting my back and talking softly and consolingly to me. I tried to understand what had happened. What was she was doing in Charlotte instead of New Orleans? Then awareness began to sink in, the horror returned and the nightmare began again.

Walking out of my bedroom, I saw my mother and my niece Jessica sleeping in the living room. Helen had taken care of bringing my family to me. In the kitchen, a freshly baked breakfast casserole was sitting on the stove. My friend Joanna, who had also been at the hospital and lived almost fifty miles away, had brought us breakfast, then left so as not to awaken the family. I wish she had stayed for a while. Joanna also left a notebook along with a message for me. I was to write down everything that was happening – the phone calls, the messages of condolences from friends, phone numbers and lists of what I needed to do in the next week. That notebook became very important to me over the next few months. I never left home without it. I have been blessed with such caring friends who were there in the beginning and for so many years to come.

My sister Theresa, known affectionately as "Aunt T," arrived from Pensacola completely devastated. She and I were very close through the years. T was always there for Pete and Mike – she helped them in so many ways. I often felt she was their "other mother," since they could confide in Aunt T the things they were not able to confide to their mom. Pete's girlfriend, Ellen, who had been on a business trip in California, was now here for Pete. My friend Kathy returned to take my project documents to my coworkers, so I would be relieved of work concerns. So many wanted to find a way to help and comfort, and they did.

The phone rang off the hook with my friends and Pete's friends asking what they could do. But, the hardest calls were the ones from Mike's friends. Theirs were calls of inexpressible grief as they cried uncontrollably and shared their love and stories of Mike. My family finally had to answer the phone and take messages, as I could no longer handle the reality of my truth. Then I received a call from Mike's dad to discuss funeral arrangements. What was the hurry? I hadn't even had time to begin to assimilate the loss much less make plans for the final farewell. I was numb and far away in a trance, trying to take in this new reality. But, I agreed to meet with him the next day at the funeral home.

That whole week was chaotic and overwhelming. On Monday, Ed and I visited the funeral home and decided Mike would be cremated after the wake and service. When I retuned home my mom and my sister Theresa were going through boxes and boxes of pictures of Mike, creating beautiful photo albums for the wake. They were there to do the things I couldn't and didn't have the time or stamina to do. Everything was happening much too fast for me.

Megan and her mom came to bring food and visit. Helen and June came back to see if I was still "here." As Helen put it, "I thought we had lost you." She was right – I was lost and would be for a long time. But, at the time, I was in the "take care of my Mikie" mode. I couldn't entirely lose it yet – I had to give all my attention to Mike and then I could go into that dark, swirling black hole. When Mike's friends came to visit, I was the one to console them, especially his best friend Adam, who broke down in tears when he entered Mike's bedroom.

On Tuesday Ed, Pete and I had to write Mike's obituary. God, that was heart-wrenching. We had to choose Mike's clothes for the wake and find a baseball cap for his scarred and wounded head. Of course, Mike would wear his white Nautica T-shirt and khaki pants with a blue Nautica short-sleeved over shirt. No suit for Mikie. He would look like he always did, the way he was known to his friends and the way he would always be remembered. We couldn't find Mike's high school baseball cap to cover his scar. His friend, Kelly, talked to their high school principal to try to get a new baseball cap, but instead, Mr. Nixon gave Kelly his very own baseball cap for Mike. He said later in a condolence note that he was honored to share a hat with Mike in eternal life. I felt that was quite a tribute.

Wednesday was D-day, the day we would wake Mike. The calls and visits continued. Ellen and her mom came with food and at least twenty laminated copies of Mike's obituary from the newspaper. Ellen's father and brother had also spent much of the night with us at the hospital. Pete was loved by Ellen's family, and Ellen had also lost an older stepbrother many years earlier. They knew the pain. My friend Alice made copies of all the songs that would be part of Mike's *Celebration of Life*, so everyone would have a copy during the service. The thoughtfulness and outpouring of love and support from so many people was overwhelming and deeply touching. I believe I got my strength from them while planning my beloved son's funeral.

My brother Chip arrived in Charlotte that day, as did Ed's family. Pete's friend, Josh, came from Knoxville with Pete's suit, to attend Mike's service and to be there for Pete. The house was chaotic, cluttered and full of people. Clothes and suitcases were strewn throughout every room. My friends, Mike and Dagmar, offered to put up Theresa and Chip for the night. They were friends from New Orleans who knew my family and I knew they would give T and Chip some comfort for their grief. My neighbor, Gwen, had my mother, my sister, Mary Lee and my niece, Jessica staying in her home. She also stayed back at my home during Mike's service to get the house in some kind of order for when friends would arrive. She prepared some sandwiches and finger food. She did those things I hadn't even thought to do.

In the afternoon, I went to the funeral home to bring the photo albums and pictures to display, along with the music I thought would be appropriate for Mike – his favorite Marvin Gaye and Otis Redding. I, for one, couldn't handle the rap songs on such an occasion, but I knew this music would bring a smile through his friends' tears. I then discovered the room we had chosen had been changed to a much larger chapel and adjoining room. One of the directors knew Mike and his friends, and he explained to the funeral home owner he knew this wake and funeral would be huge. Was he right!

Wednesday evening the doors to the chapel were opened early because a long line was already forming outside. Ed, Pete and I stood in the reception room receiving each and every person non-stop for hours. We were asked to hurry the greetings, as the line outside the funeral home was now two blocks long. There was only time for hugs and a few brief words from all who came to express their condolences and sorrow for our loss. Several of Mike's girl friends brought me roses and cards with handwritten notes about how much Mike meant to them. As we stood in the receiving line, the real wake was actually taking place in the parking lot. There, Mike's friends were crying and consoling each other. Some made phone calls to friends still in Wilmington. It was the first day of classes for the new semester and many were grieved that they were not able to be in Charlotte with Mike. Mike's grandmother exclaimed she had never seen so many grown men cry. That's where I wanted to be, at the real wake.

Finally, the long line came to an end, and I went to stand by Mike's coffin. I was overwhelmed and brought to tears to discover that he was covered in red roses. There was a golf ball with a touching message from a friend, a letter and ski goggles from Aunt T, who taught the boys how to ski, a gold ring, letters to Mike and so many more meaningful objects of affection. I was touched and grateful. What a loving tribute to my son. I had never seen anything like this and I cried at the outpouring of the love for their "brother" from his family and "family of friends." Many stayed a while to talk and share stories. We all had a few tearful laughs remembering our Mike and how he lived in the moment. It was hard to leave my beautiful son alone in that coffin, but the tokens of affection helped to comfort me – Mike was not alone.

The song *Angel*, by Sarah McLachlan, filled the silence as the pallbearers walked with Mike's coffin into the chapel the next morning. This was the song Mike had played over and over again, as he sat alone in his room, mourning the tragic death of a friend a few years earlier. Many of his friends were surprised because they had wanted to tell me that was the song they felt should be played, but didn't feel they had the right to do so. I guess Mike had us all in sync. My colleague, Joan, gave the gift of her beautiful voice and sang a few requested songs. Some of Mike's friends spoke and my sister, Mary Lee, read a poignant poem. I got up to speak and felt as though I just rambled on, but Megan told me later I just looked lost. I did share a letter Mike left for me in a textbook when I was finishing my degree. In it he said, "For every dark night there's a brighter day ahead." I still hold that message close to my heart.

By far, the most touching and heartbreaking words came in the eulogy given by my son, Pete. Mikie's older brother delivered these beautiful, heart-wrenching words the very last time we saw Mike's face. Pete stood at the podium so proud of his little brother. He spoke these words through tears, as he hunched over the podium so devastated. He spoke from the depths of his heart. He spoke from the depths of an eerie fog he had never known before. He spoke to the hundreds of family and friends that loved Mike so dearly. He spoke, knowing that he, nor anyone who knew Mike, would ever be the same again.

Our Mikey

To Mikey:

I can't really put anything into words that could ever be worthy of my baby brother. He was the most selfless, caring, thoughtful, and loving person I've ever known. Anyone who truly knew him would agree. If he could do something to make someone he cared about happy, he wouldn't hesitate, regardless of how much it cost or what he had to do to do it. There were several Christmases and birthdays where he didn't know how he would pay his bills, but as long as he had gotten everybody nice gifts, he didn't care. Looking back on the countless pictures and memories, I know that he made the last twenty-two years of my life the best they will ever be.

Ever since he was just a baby, I tried to protect him and look out for him. It really drove him nuts sometimes. When we were kids, our family had a house on the Tangipahoa River in Louisiana. There was this cliff near the water's edge that I always used to have nightmares about, and anytime he would go anywhere near it, I would go berserk. I wouldn't care how frustrated or upset he got, just as long as he was safe. Just last weekend, we were riding the waves at the beach, and the current and undertow was really strong. I kept irritating the hell out of him, because I wouldn't let him stray more than ten feet from me.

I felt as though it was my duty to see that he never felt any pain or hurt. As we were growing up, I would even try to beat up anyone who hurt his feelings or picked on him in the slightest way. That was kind of tough, since it certainly wasn't hard to hurt his feelings. He could be so damn sensitive. However, that sincere sensitivity wasn't just directed towards himself. If anyone he cared about was going through a hard time, it was as though he felt their pain as deeply as they did. He genuinely cared about others.

He was obviously an extraordinary and wonderful human being, but he was also the best little brother a guy could ever have. Mikey and I would always be there for each other through good times and bad. If I ever needed him for anything, I could always count on him. I would like to think *he felt the same. He certainly felt that he could count on me to buy him, and his friends, beer when we were younger. I used to give them a hard time about that, but it always made me feel good to come through for him.*

I could also always count on him to be the first person to tell me how proud he was of me, and it really always felt so good to hear him say it. Something like that is really special when it comes from someone you truly admired. I hope he knows just how proud of him I was and still am. How could anyone not be proud of someone who had such a generous and caring soul, a solid work ethic, great athletic talent, and the respect and admiration of so many of his peers. I can remember going to see one of his high school baseball games. As I was walking to the stands, a baseball landed about thirty feet from me behind the fence. Mikey had just hit a homerun. When I got to the stands, it felt so good to tell everyone, "That was my brother." That was just one of countless moments when he made me proud to be his brother.

I feel so lucky and fortunate to have someone so beautiful be a part of my life for the last twenty-two years. I, and obviously so many others, loved him dearly, and he will be sorely missed. I can't imagine what kind of God would allow something like this to happen. I would just like to think his soul was just too good for this earth.

I LOVE YOU, MIKEY!!!

Shattered

One day our lives were fine,
Time for you finally seemed better,
Then one step, one second in time
And then everything just shattered.
You were here, your laughter,
Your smile,
Your smell,
Then one step, one second in time
And then everything just shattered.
The things I miss I never dreamed I would,
The worry, the clock, the endless nights,
Then one step, one second in time
And then everything just shattered.
The words you spoke that morning,
Will forever be in my heart,
Have a good day Mom, I love you.
Then one step, one second in time
And then everything just shattered.
The call,
The shock, the fear, the ride to be with you,
After one step, one second in time
When everything just shattered.
I held your hand,
I kissed your face, I told you that I loved you.
Did you hear me?
After that step, that second in time
When everything just shattered.
I cry for you, I still kiss your face,
My heart will forever be broken.

Did you know how this would end?
When you took that step, your second in time
When my world just shattered.
I miss you now,
I always will . . .
Until I take my step, my second in time
When the pieces all fit together.

By Lisa Roark

Signs from Mike

Almost immediately after he transitioned, Mike began sending me signs, but it took me a little while to figure it out. Luckily, I had help from friends who recognized what was happening and validated the occurrences I found so unusual.

Within the first two weeks, strange things were happening all around me, especially in the kitchen. The kitchen clock stopped, the coffee maker died for no apparent reason, one side of the toaster quit working and light bulbs burned out all over the house. As soon as I replaced one bulb, another would go out. While talking with my friend Joanna, I told her all the things happening around the house that I found so very unusual. Her first reaction was, "It's Mike!" She was amazed at how soon Mike had come through and stressed that it was rare to have a loved one come through so early. "He must be very well adjusted on the Other Side," she exclaimed. I stopped changing the light bulbs and let the last one remain dark. Once I understood, the lights stopped going out, for a while anyway. My Mikie was letting me know he was close by and was orchestrating these happenings with his energy.

I had kept a red rose from Mike's casket and hung it to dry on my bathroom mirror. Two others were hanging on the other side of the mirror for Pete. There were no air vents close by, yet petals began falling from my rose, but *only* when I was standing at the mirror, never when I was out of the room. Once, six fell at the same time – just from my rose; not one petal ever fell from Pete's roses. Again, Mike was telling me, "I'm here with you, Mom." That was Mike's style, communicating with roses. He was always buying them for the ladies. I still have the one he gave me on my birthday, the week before his accident. We were catching a flight to Pensacola for a family reunion and to celebrate my birthday and my sister Theresa's birthday (we were born on the same day, two years apart). Mike was running late from a golf game with his friend Lou. In he walked with one red rose – the kind you find at the convenient marts – and with his charming smile and charismatic air, he explained he was late because he had to stop to buy me a red rose for my birthday. He sure did have his momma wrapped! That rose sits in a vase on my "Mikie Shrine". Little did I know then how much comfort it would bring to me.

Three weeks after the accident, I woke up in the middle of the night with a pen in my hand. I was lying on my stomach, my hand under the pillow, and I was very confused. I was holding the pen exactly as if I had been writing. I realized this was the third night this had happened. Writing has always been the way I figure things out, and my way of dealing with problems. Mike knew this. I felt Mike was reminding me to write and guiding me to deal with my grief. I grabbed some paper from my night table and began writing in the dark, something I had learned in a dream class years before. I started by writing questions to Mike, letting him know I was listening. The responses I received were, "Momma" and "Wait for me." My pen wrote the words. There were no words in my head or voices from the past. My hand was just guided in the dark. It was to be another year before I understood his message.

The next day Kathy and Helen joined me on my journey to Highway 218 to meet the medic who arrived at the scene to aid Mike the night of the accident, and who would guide us to the site. Pete had been very adamant that I not go. I believe Pete had already been there, and I didn't want to upset him, but witnessing where Mike was thrown from the car was something I felt strongly I needed to do. I waited until Pete returned to Knoxville before embarking on my mission. On the way, we stopped at a florist to purchase a red rose for Mike, and as we pulled away, *Angel* began playing on the car radio. Tears poured down my cheeks and I felt as if Mike wanted me to see where he really died. When we reached the site with the medic, I finally understood why it took so long for the police and medics to reach him and why no 911 calls were made. I now understood why I received *that* phone call from a stranger the night that life, as I knew it, came to an end. It was in the middle of nowhere; there was no shoulder on the narrow, curving road and the ravine was overgrown with brush and trees, except for the place where Mikie came to lay. Now I could see why they had a hard time finding Mike. He was forcefully thrown a great distance as the car split in half.

We stayed there quite a while and placed our flowers on the blood-soaked towel where Mike's head laid, where two men sat with him and administered first aid until the medics arrived. We prayed and we cried together surrounded by so many rain and blood-soaked blankets and towels left by caring strangers. I felt we left the site of Mike's last minutes in this world a much more peaceful place.

On the way home we stopped at a bookstore in Monroe to buy a journal for my letters to Mike. It happened to be the same chain as the bookstore in Charlotte where I bought a journal for Pete before he returned to Knoxville. The very same man was at the counter and when I asked him if he worked in the Charlotte store, he said yes. He added it was unusual for him to be there, but for some reason he had been asked to help out at the Monroe store that day. Coincidence? I don't think so. I began writing to Mike every night, but by spring, I was only writing occasionally. The daily writing became too hard and I needed to go into my place of denial for a while. The depression and grief were relentless.

Before Pete left for Knoxville, Ellen and Megan came over for dinner. I knew this would be very difficult for all of us. I hadn't cooked since Mike left and I had a very hard time just going to the grocery store. I would pick up Mike's favorite foods and lemon flavored bottled water before realizing there was no reason to buy them anymore. The first time I went to the store after Mike's accident, I broke into tears as soon as I entered the produce section and saw the bags of raw carrots. I fled, leaving the grocery basket in the aisle, and returned home empty handed. Mike would eat raw carrots and dip when he came home from work, while waiting for dinner. He didn't need them anymore.

I knew that dinner was important for all of us. It had to be special, and it would be an honor to Mike. While purchasing pork chops, I noticed a lady standing next to me. The woman started a conversation about the filet mignon on sale that week and how great they were. Let me just say I have never purchased filet mignon at the grocery store. It was always too expensive. I had already chosen some very nice pork chops and was finished in the meat department. But this woman would not let me walk away; she was determined I should purchase the filet mignon. When I finally relented, placed the pork chops back in the cooler and picked up the package of filet mignon, she went on her way and didn't say another word. It was as if she had never spoken. I said, "Okay, Mikie, you want us to have the best, so we'll have filet mignon for your dinner tonight." He did like the good things in life.

Six weeks after Mike transitioned, Joanna told me about an open session regarding *Messages from the Other Side* with the psychic-medium Mary Beth Wrenn. Several of my friends agreed, and were very eager, to attend with me. The room held about fifty people, all longing to hear from loved ones. I was disappointed we had to sit toward the back; I thought I would be in a better position if I were in the front row. Was I wrong!

The session began with Mary Beth pointing directly to me and stating that there was a huge blue and white ball of energy right over my head. Blue was Mike's favorite color. I knew it was Mike. I was so in awe and excited by my experience, I went directly to my Mikie journal when I returned home and wrote the following:

Mary Beth said that you were very honest and religious, although I've always thought of you as more spiritual and one who was seeking answers. We always discussed other possibilities about life and the Other Side. She saw you as a counselor with initials behind your name. You did want to be a psychologist when you first began your studies at college, but you were not a book person and felt defeated. When I talked to Mary Beth at the break I told her how you were always there for your friends, especially the girls, who could talk to you about their feelings or the ones who had problems or were troubled. Mary Beth just said, "Duhh!"

Helen, June, Alice and Dagmar were with me and they all told me when Mary Beth said she saw you as a counselor they thought, "That's Mike!" They knew you too. Then she said, "He's very proud of you and you've just had a major change in your life." Dagmar grabbed my hand and repeated, "It's Mike!" We all knew you were trying to let me know you were still with me. Mary Beth said you were right behind me; you were all this warmth giving me love. You were telling me you weren't really gone; you were always with me and would be forever in my heart. But then came the hard part. Mary Beth said I had all this "stuff" in the way and I was blocking you out of my heart. I know you must mean the anger that is starting to take over and the pain I feel when I think of you not being here.

Mary Beth tried to leave me and go on to others but she said you wouldn't let her. That was just like you, when you

41

wanted to say something; you were always determined to be heard! Respect was always so important to you. She tried to focus her energy on the other side of the room, but you are something else! You wanted to comfort your mom and let her know you were okay. Mary Beth said she saw an accident and saw the left side of the neck was cut, which no one really knew, because all the focus was on your head injuries. Then she mentioned a car accident and said, "MEL?" Your initials – Michael Edward Ludman. MEL was also on the key chain I had given you for Christmas that was never found. I blurted out, "That's my son!" She asked about a girl in the car with you and said it wasn't her fault; I had to forgive and release her from the guilt. She had to be talking about Serena; she was driving that night.

Then Mary Beth saw a strong, red energy (love) and said it wasn't her fault things didn't work out between the two of you. I knew that part was about you and Megan. You also wanted her to let go of her feelings of guilt. Later, Mary Beth asked me how long it had been since you passed. When I told her a little over six weeks, she was stunned. She said it's rare to be able to communicate so soon and she added you definitely had a very strong, influential personality on the Other Side. When we talked again on another break, she said you are a wonderful person, but a bit of a loudmouth and bossy. You wouldn't let her go. All I could say was, "Yes, that's my Mikie!" She also saw you above me, which symbolized that you were always looking out for me, trying to protect me and take care of me. During the break strangers came to me with hugs, some close to tears, and told me they could feel the love from you in the room and they were in awe of what had happened between us that evening.

42

When the session ended, the Woo Woos (my family of friends) *presented me with a beautiful and meaningful gift. It was a garden stone with two open hands and the inscription, "Until we meet again find peace in heaven's hands." The stone included a bronze plate reading, "My Mike, Your loving spirit fills my heart."*

I was in another world as I drove home that night. There was no doubt among my friends, the people in the session or with Mary Beth that Mike was there. In the next few months, Mary Beth came to know Mike quite well. During a private session, she told me about Mike's friend, who also died in an auto accident eight months later and shared much more about Mike's accident. In fact, in the following months, other psychic-mediums gave me very vivid details about his accident. People may doubt, but when the messages are so clear and insightful, I know there are individuals with the gift who can connect to the Other Side. I found that although they connect, they can only explain what they see or hear within their own perception and the messages are ours to figure out. Sometimes it takes awhile. Some messages are only significant to a particular person and no one else.

I will never forget that first session and will never doubt what Mike tries to communicate. When I joined KinderMourn, I was reassured to learn many parents went to mediums and was encouraged to do what I felt I needed to do. It was also important to find an authentic psychic-medium. It only took a short time in a session to know. I went to different psychics for quite a while until I finally realized that all the messages Mike gave me through dreams and through signs were the evolvement of a new communication between Mike and me that would continue for my lifetime.

During the weeks that followed, I received four very strange phone messages that came during the night. I never checked for messages first thing in the morning, but for some reason, I picked up the receiver. There were no blinking lights on the phone – I had to dial a number to check the voicemail. The messages contained very high-pitched chirping sounds, slow chirping sounds, nothing remotely like a fax machine. The calls were very eerie. In fact, the calls were so odd I finally wondered if it was Mike. I would continue to listen and the high-pitched chirping would go on and on until I finally hung up.

One night, while reading a book by the psychic-medium Sylvia Browne, I read a section where she referred to messages from the Other Side sometimes coming through as high-pitched chirping sounds. My hair stood up on the back of my neck. All I could think was, "Oh my God! I hung up on Mikie!" When I told Pete about the calls, he suggested I save the next message on tape and ask Mary Beth if she could decipher it. Of course, the calls never came again. I started to see a pattern. As soon as I figured out what Mike was doing, he would stop. I believe there was no specific message; he only wanted me to know he was always around me and wanted me to be aware.

I now understood and I began to take those signs from Mike as an everyday occurrence. I sensed that we were developing a communication with each other on some other level. I then understood too, sometimes Mike was just "messing" with me. I could see him smiling and laughing his low, mischievous laugh he laughed when he "Got ya!"

I believe that's what he did with his tennis shoes. When Mike left for Wilmington, he had on his new tennis shoes and left his other pair perfectly lined up in front of his dresser. That's the way they remained for years, except when he moved them around. The first time I saw the change in the shoes I dropped to my knees and cried. The right shoe was a little behind and to the right of the left shoe, as if someone had taken a step toward his closet. I hadn't been through his closet yet and felt strongly as if there was something he wanted me to find. I wouldn't find out what it was until later, when I visited another psychic-medium named Jan.

During the session with Jan I refrained from revealing anything about the shoe episodes, but she told me Mike said I was looking for a little book that was in a box on the floor in his closet. By this time, I had already been through his closet and didn't understand the message. When I returned home, I immediately went to Mike's room to search the closet again. At the bottom of a box I had already searched, I found the instruction book to Mike's cordless telephone still in the plastic envelope. After Mike left, I unplugged his phone, because I didn't know how operate it. I kept saying to myself, "I wish I had asked Mike how to use the phone when he was here." I always took it for granted that as long as he knew the ins and outs of the phone so well, I wouldn't have to bother with all this new machine stuff. He's the only one who knew I wanted to learn how to operate his phone.

Mike moved his shoes around pretty often in those first few years, but not as much anymore. Now that I understood, I'd just say, "Hello" and thank him for coming. I know he's only reassuring me he's with me and loves me. He did the same thing with lights, especially the lights above the kitchen sink. My mother pointed out that Mike bought and installed the kitchen sink for me as a surprise when I returned to the university to complete my degree and graduated in December 1999. He was very proud of my accomplishment and had been very encouraging as I worked to complete that part of my life. Now I could never leave those lights on when I left the house, as I had done previously, because now I felt I would return to a dark house. I had to activate living room lamps when I wanted to make sure I'd have light when I returned home at night.

Mike has "messed" with me in so many ways. Of course, things never occur if I'm looking for them. Those special occurrences only happen when he can catch me off guard. He did, and still does, a good job of that.

Mike had always worn his long gold chain with the cross, his gold matching bracelet and watch. After the accident his broken watch was the only piece of jewelry the police gave me in that God-awful baggie, along with Mike's lighter, some loose change and his belt. A few days after the accident, his friends, Sean, Lou and Nick went back out to the site and found Mike's gold chain and bracelet. That alone was a miracle, considering the overgrown brush in that area. They never found the gold cross he had worn on the chain.

At the time, I decided to keep his gold chain and gave the bracelet to Pete. Pete never wore jewelry, only his watch, but he wore Mike's bracelet every day and never took it off for a very long time. It wasn't until the clasp broke for the second time that I suggested Mike was trying to tell him something – to let go and move on. I had placed Mike's chain neatly in his jewelry box next to his broken watch, just as he would have done. One day I decided to begin wearing his chain. When I opened the jewelry box, the chain was all bunched up in a corner instead of neatly laid where I had placed it. Surely, Mike was acknowledging me wearing it.

While at work one day, I received a message on my cell phone from Ed saying he was returning my phone call from earlier in the day. I had been in meetings and had not telephoned Ed. He said my phone number was on his cell phone from earlier that morning. I had not made the call. Later in the day, I received a call from my mother in New Orleans. Mom was excited and perplexed by what had happened to her during the day. She had an emergency need of a plumber and finally located one who would come to the house in the afternoon. When she answered the door, she gasped. The young plumber looked so much like Mike. Mom said the young man diligently went to work on the problem and then sat down with her to discuss the bill. She asked him his name and he answered, "Mike." Mom finally told him a little about our Mike and he listened intently, then left. She felt our Mike had definitely sent "Mike the plumber" to her home that day.

A few days later I received a phone call from Megan. She was thrilled, yet mystified by what had happened. She felt the need to share it with me since she knew I would understand. Megan had randomly taken the name of a child off the Angel Tree at the mall to help a less fortunate child to whom she would send presents for Christmas. When she opened the envelope she discovered the name of a little girl. Her name was Nautica! That was no coincidence. Mike only wore Nautica clothes and cologne, and who ever heard of a child named Nautica!? She and I both believed Mike sent her that child to reassure her that he was with her and looking over her. Some things we will never know for sure, but we certainly cannot doubt the obvious. Megan was definitely beginning to believe all the messages and coincidences were not really coincidences at all – they were contacts and gifts from Mike.

There were times, I'm not sure why, when Mike would close the door to his bedroom. The first time he closed the door my sister, Theresa, was with me. She came to stay with me for a weekend a few months after the accident and we had just arrived home from the airport. I wanted to show her something in Mike's room, and as we turned the hall corner, I saw his closed bedroom door. I always left the door open. If Mike was telling us to stay out of his room, I wasn't honoring his request. I don't think anything will make me stay out of his room. But, I understood what he was trying to say. I know he wants me to go on with my life, to embrace life and live life for him and Pete and to be happy. He'll have to be patient with me on that one.

There were many evenings when I fell asleep crying on Mike's bed. I felt I had to be near his essence, and I had kept everything in his room exactly as it was when he left. I could still smell his scent on his sheets and pillows as I sobbed like a wounded child. One evening, as I turned off his bedside lamp, I looked up and saw the light-illuminated stars I had given him years before. I never realized he had placed them on his ceiling. They could only be seen once the light was out and then shone brightly for only a few minutes. That night I laughed through the tears. I felt as if I was in the sky floating with my Mikie – a place I so desperately wanted to be. Those stars brought me comfort and yet let me know how little I sometimes understood my son, especially his sentimental, childlike side. I wanted to embrace and hold the moment forever. Then the stars dimmed and I was back in that unimaginable, painful, grief-stricken reality.

Although I felt Mike and I were developing our own manner of communication, I couldn't resist the desire to be a part of an open session by the internationally known psychic-medium, John Edward, when he made an appearance in Charlotte a few months later. Of course, it was Helen who found tickets for us and her daughter Lynn. There were thousands of people in attendance, and we were seated in the back, too far to be noticed, or so I thought. I suddenly realized a colleague and his wife were sitting in the row in front of us. She was there to hear from her dad, who died shortly before her marriage. Well, as the session continued, John Edward pointed in our immediate area and said he had someone who was married shortly after her dad died and who shot fireworks after a very significant death. He added that the number "23" was very significant. I understood about the fireworks – my father died on New Year's Eve in 1999 and that day was very special to him – everyone went to the Muller's (my maiden name) house for New Year's Eve to enjoy a magnificent fireworks display. The night my father died, Mike and I went out in the backyard and he set off a few fireworks at midnight in honor of his grandfather, my dad. I was trying to figure out the "23" – Mike would now be twenty-three-years-old, but the marriage part of the message was meant for my colleague's wife. Earlier in the session, John Edward explained that sometimes messages from different spirits try to come through together when those in the audience are seated near each other. I was talking with Helen, trying to figure out if it was Mike and didn't hear John Edward ask, "Who's Mikie?" By then, other people were claiming the message for themselves, but John Edward said no. He finally moved on to others.

When I was asked later why I didn't raise my hand when Edward asked, "Who's Mikie?" I started to cry. I realized I had missed him. After the session I drove directly to the cemetery to be with Mike and called Megan. She couldn't believe I didn't understand it was Mike – Mike's number for his phone codes, etc. was "23". I even used Mikie23 as the password on my computer. I'd heard about *psychic amnesia* and realized I failed to recognize Mikie – he tried so hard to reach me amongst thousands of people, and I missed him. I was devastated. I'd let Mike down. I'd missed my chance. I cried all the way to the cemetery and asked Mike to forgive me.

I couldn't sleep that night, and the next day I went to see Mary Beth during my lunch hour. She also attended the John Edward's session. She explained several things Mike was showing her and said he was there on Sunday, organizing spirits on the Other Side. For some reason, Mike ended by showing Mary Beth a football, which made no sense to me.

The next morning I had a meeting which took place in a conference room on the 22nd floor. The room was surrounded by open glass that overlooked downtown Charlotte. As I took my place at the conference table, I noticed the young man sitting next to me was wearing all Nautica clothing. As the meeting opened, a hawk began gliding on air currents outside the window, back and forth, as if entertaining the whole group. It was hard to stay focused on the discussion. The hawk had become a symbol of Mike (but that's another story). Then, out of the blue, one of my teammates held up a football with a company logo on it and asked bewildered, "Where did this football come from?" I laughed to myself and smiled throughout the meeting. Maybe it was Mike's way of saying, "It's okay, Mom – I can communicate with you anywhere." He wasn't going to let me beat myself up for not recognizing his contact on Sunday. Those special moments mean so much to me as I learn to live in my new reality.

Mike continues to give me these little signs – but not as often as he used to. Now the signs are less obvious. I feel he understands that I understand, that I've grown and I'm more aware. Now the signs are guiding me on my way, helping me to heal, helping me make decisions, and encouraging me to accept where he is and to learn how to communicate with him on another level.

Dreading Today

I wake up now every morning,
Dreading the start of each new day.
I have such a fear of just not knowing
What will happen next along my way.
What will this day bring,
Will it be as bad as the day before,
Or will it somehow hold a peace
That will stay in my heart forevermore.
Will I struggle to hold back tears,
Or will there be a smile for me today.
Will a friend be there for me
To help me along my way.
Or will I face this day alone,
And not know which direction that I should go.
Will I hold this pain inside
Or will it somehow have to show.
Will I make it until tomorrow,
Will someone I love walk out that door
To never come back home to me
To be gone forevermore.
With everyday that passes by,
My fear just grows and grows,
Because what will happen through this day
God in Heaven only knows.

So if I make it until tomorrow,
I know it will start the exact same way.
I will be so fearful of just not knowing
What will happen next along my way.

By Lisa Roark

It's Too Big!

During the months following Mike's accident, life was too overwhelming for me to even function. It was surreal – like being entombed in a Dali painting. People expected me to "Get on with my life" or to "Snap out of it" or tell me, "You should be over it by now," or the really big one, "He's in a better place!" My belief in humanity began to wane, and I yearned to be as far away from reality as possible. The panic attacks began. I feared being alone, yet I wanted to be alone – to be left totally alone. I couldn't think or communicate or be "on." I was numb. I cried uncontrollably, with little provocation, usually just blindsided with no warning. I longed to spend all my time at the cemetery taking care of my son, fussing over him in the only way left to me now. Pete put it all in perspective one day when he said, "It's too big, it's just too big!"

Life was the nightmare. I recall waking one morning and looking around my room, disoriented. Then I remembered where I was and realized it was in the waking hours of reality that the real nightmare continued. I wished I could just take a pill and sleep through it, sleep through the rest of my life if possible. There was no way to deal with the pain as I walked around each day trying to appear *normal*. Vicki Windham's poem, *What is Normal Now?* describes the surrealism of this unbearable state of grief when she says:

> *"Normal is hiding all the things that have become 'normal' for you to feel, so that everyone around you will think you are NORMAL."*

What most people can never understand is that no one survives the death of a child and remains unchanged. As Stephanie Ericsson wrote in *Companion Through Darkness*:

> *"Grief is a tidal wave that overtakes you, smashes down upon you with unimaginable force, sweeps you up into its darkness, where you tumble and crash against unidentifiable surfaces only to be thrown out on an unknown beach, bruised, reshaped."*

A simple task like driving was beyond my capabilities. My mind was so far away in another dimension, and so far removed from reality, that just getting to work was overwhelming. I became lost driving the same route I had driven every day for years. Suddenly I'd become aware I had no idea how I had arrived at a certain place along the way. Everything appeared different. The exit ramps of the interstate were puzzling and confusing. Landmarks seemed out of place. A person in such grief should never be allowed to drive alone or even do something as simple as go to the grocery alone. It's just too big!

Ericsson warned:

"Grief makes what others think of you moot. It shears away the masks of normal life and forces brutal honesty out of your mouth before propriety can stop you. It shoves away friends and scares away so-called friends and rewrites your address book for you."

Grief did unimaginable damage to my life. My address book did change. There were friends who, for whatever reason, drifted by the wayside. I don't know if they couldn't handle my pain or couldn't allow it. Thank God there were true friends who were there for me throughout the many months and years that followed. It was their little kindnesses and thoughtful remembrances that were so heartwarming and healing. Some just showed up unannounced to let me know they were there and weren't leaving me. Others came at a moment's notice, no questions asked. They sat with me, listened to me and comforted me. Sometimes it was only the idea of their presence that was so comforting. There were those who spent weekends with me, stayed overnight, gave healing massages, invited me to dinners, sent cards, left beautiful, encouraging phone messages, cut the grass, spent time at the cemetery with me, brought me books about grief and healing, and when the time was right, there were those who came to laugh and play and to persuade me to embrace life again. Each and every one had their own way and each and every way was so helpful, so meaningful and so relevant.

Being an avid reader, I was now only interested in reading about life after death and how to communicate with my son. Other cultures do a much better job of addressing grief and allowing the grief-stricken time to mourn. I learned that the death of a child and the grief of a parent are actually ritualized in many countries. I read about them in Carol Staudacher's book, *Beyond Grief: A Guide for Recovering from the Death of a Loved One.* She cites that the Yakurr of Nigeria believe that after death, a child continues to live with the family in a different form and some parents even leave food for their child outside the front door. In Bali, it's common for parents to visit a Balinese shaman and healer, one trained and capable of going into a trance state to contact the child's spirit. Once the child's spirit enters the shaman's body the parents can talk to their child. In Brazil, the Umbanda followers conduct a ritual in which the spirits of the dead children are "called" and many parents bring wrapped candy or toys for their child. If you remember the movie *It's A Wonderful Life,* you will recall that George Bailey was still wearing a black armband six months after the death of his father. In each of these instances, people are allowed to grieve openly. Our society doesn't allow that anymore.

I found the workplace to be ill equipped to handle such devastating grief. There were times when I broke into tears and just left for the day. I couldn't concentrate. Things I did previously without thinking, now seemed hard to comprehend. Every keystroke on the computer felt like a foreign language. I know I made the whole office uncomfortable because they didn't know how to deal with my emotional state. No one there knew firsthand what it felt like to lose a child. Most of my co-workers felt more comfortable avoiding me and keeping their distance. The director gave me tasks which isolated me and minimized my involvement with the team. Unfortunately, it diminished my self-esteem at the most vulnerable time of my life. Through what I learned in my grief group, KinderMourn, I began to forgive and realize they were the "clueless people." It wasn't their fault.

Many people who experience the sudden death of a child are also diagnosed with Post Traumatic Stress Disorder (PTSD). I realized I was in such a place. I had been lifted out of my world and dropped into an unfamiliar universe. I suffered from low self-esteem and felt disconnected. I found myself saying repeatedly, "I just want my life back!" I constantly relived the events and couldn't sleep without sleeping pills prescribed by my psychiatrist. Every time I closed my eyes, the movies started to play – the long night with Mike as his body slowly died. I had seen and heard so much about his accident that I felt I was actually there, and those scenes played in my head too. Then the other movies crept in – the ones in which I looked back and relived the moments with Mike where I regretted things I said or did, which I could no longer make right. I was always "on guard," feeling irritable, angry, sad, and easily startled and overcome by tears. I suffered panic attacks just thinking about Mike or by an event that triggered a certain memory of Mike.

One night while changing channels on the television (at that time I referred to it as the babysitter for the numb), I caught part of a movie with Walter Matthau portraying a character in the hospital who was obviously dying. Before

I could turn the station, I heard the piercing blip, blip, blip of the heart monitor. My panic rose to such a high level of distress that I called a friend who lived nearby. I couldn't breathe, I couldn't stop the tears, I couldn't stop the pain in my heart. Yes, my heart did physically hurt. When Dagmar arrived, she sat and held me while I calmed down and described to her the cause for this attack. I couldn't think of the name of the movie, but Dagmar jogged my memory – the movie was *Hanging Up!* My God! My mind made the connection. Those phone calls that came in the night with the high-pitched chirping sounds, were actually the sounds of the blips of a heart monitor. I really did hang up on Mikie.

I withdrew from my friends and only wanted to be with Pete. But Pete lived four hours away and was struggling with his own grief. For the first year or two, we talked on the phone and visited as often as we could. I felt as if I was wandering around lost, only going through the motions of living. I lost interest in everyday events and activities I previously enjoyed. I tried unsuccessfully to deaden myself physically and mentally in order to avoid my emotional death. I became a "used-to-be."

Visits to psychics became a new activity in my life to help me function and to find a way to be in contact with Mike. Staudacher, in *Beyond Grief,* writes that going to a medium or psychic can take us from the physical to the metaphysical. She states:

> *"The more we communicate with our child even after he is gone and with the professionals who can satisfy our need to understand the physical aspects of his death, and with one another, in developing an atmosphere in which healing is easier the bigger the*

language grows. And the bigger the language, the more possible it becomes to answer our most urgent questions after our child's death."

These visits were bittersweet – so much I understood and yet so much I didn't understand until months or even years later. I had a support network that kept me putting one foot in front of the other and made the motions of living more bearable – the psychics, KinderMourn, my psychologist and my psychiatrist (whom I still see – he prescribed anti-depressants, anti-anxiety pills and my faithful sleeping pills, without which I would have lost my mind). These people and my devoted friends and family saved my life. And, of course, Pete. He was suffering such pain and loss without any of the help I had found. It was so confusing. I wanted to be with both of my children – again, I just wanted my life back!

Without Brian, my psychologist, I can't image how I would have survived. He really listened to me and seemed to understand that all the signs and coincidences I was experiencing were real. His office was my private place to talk it out, to cry and to deal with my grief and my guilt. I always felt guilty for things I did or said to Mike that were harsh or strict, but were just parenting responsibilities, which otherwise I would never have regretted. But one very painful memory kept me distraught. About a year before Mike died, each time I heard the song *Angel* playing on the radio, I would have a vision of him as a young man in his long-sleeved, maroon dress shirt, lying in a casket. And each time I sobbed uncontrollably. The pain felt so real. It was Brian who finally convinced me that my premonition did not make me responsible for Mike's death. He explained that I had experienced precognition

– a form of extrasensory perception, in which you have prior knowledge of an event. That relieved my guilt but also alarmed me at the same time. I had seen my son's death! In the three years I met with him, Brian never discouraged me from seeing psychics or reading books to find ways to be close to Mike.

I remember a short session with a psychic at a Mind, Body and Spirit Festival three months before Mike's accident. After patiently waiting for the previous client to complete her twenty-minute reading, I finally sat down and was very impressed with the information the psychic relayed to me. She was accurate with my relationships and my personality style. Then suddenly she looked at me with a very disturbed expression and told me the sitting was over. Just like that! She told her assistant she had to leave for a while. I was only with her about ten minutes and was a little perturbed that she ended the reading so abruptly. Looking back, I realize she saw what was about to happen. I believe she saw the grief, trauma and pain that lay in my future. Thank God she excused herself. I respect her for not sharing that information.

In January, I had a private session with Jan, who told me Mike had a message for his brother. Mike said Pete "was messing up," and was telling him to "snap out of it!" The words sounded exactly like Mike. I so hoped Pete would find the kind of support network I had, but as hard as he tried, it just didn't materialize. He finally contacted a grief support group, but when he arrived at the designated time, no one was there. He did see a doctor a few times who prescribed medication to help his anxiety and sleeplessness. Pete is a very private person and not one to discuss his pain and grief with friends. He was trying to be "normal" for the outside world.

Several of Pete's friends were so worried about him that they called his Aunt T. Pete was hanging out with a guy who went out every night drinking and partying. His friends told my sister it wasn't that they thought Pete was trying to commit suicide; it was as if he just didn't care about anything anymore. He was jeopardizing his career as an architect, the one he loved and enjoyed so much. Theresa called him every day for two weeks, and all the anger bottled up in Pete was directed at her as she tried to help. He knew Aunt T would still love him no matter what, and in the end, she "guilted" him into straightening up. She sent him boxing gloves and Pete hit the punching bag in the gym so hard he knocked it out of the ceiling!

I was troubled that I hadn't known what Pete was going through. My sister's answer made sense, yet hurt at the same time. She said everyone knew I was having trouble just taking care of myself and I wasn't capable of dealing with this grief-driven episode in Pete's life. She was right, but I still felt distraught that I couldn't be there to help him.

Pete was right – it was just too big for both of us.

What Is Normal Now?

By Vicki Windham, NE Platte NE Chapter TCF (The Compassionate Friends)

NORMAL is trying to decide what to take to the cemetery for Christmas, birthdays, Valentine's Day and Easter.

NORMAL is feeling like you know how to act and are more comfortable with a funeral than a wedding or a birthday party. Yet, feeling a stab of pain in your heart when you smell the flowers, see the casket and all the crying people.

NORMAL is feeling like you can't sit another minute without screaming because you just don't like to sit through church anymore. And yet at the same time feeling like you have more faith in God than you ever had before.

NORMAL is having tears waiting behind every smile when you realize someone important is missing from all the important events in your family's life.

NORMAL is not sleeping very well because a thousand "what ifs" go through your head constantly.

NORMAL is having the TV on the minute you walk in the house to have some "noise" because the silence is deafening.

NORMAL is telling the story of your child's death as if it were an everyday common event and then gasping in horror at how awful it sounds. And yet realizing it has become a part of normal conversation.

NORMAL is each year coming up with the difficult task of how to honor your child's memory and their birthdays and surviving those days. And trying to find a balloon or flag that fits the occasion, "Happy Birthday?" Not really!

NORMAL is a new friendship with another bereaved parent and meeting over coffee and talking and crying together over your children. And worrying together over the surviving children.

NORMAL is being too tired to care if you paid the bills, cleaned the house, did the laundry or if there is any food in the house.

NORMAL is wondering this time whether you are going to say you have two or three children because you will never see this person again, and is it worth explaining that one of them has passed away. And yet, when you say two children to avoid the problem you feel horrible as if you have betrayed your child.

NORMAL is hiding all the things that have become "normal" for you to feel, so that everyone around you will think you are "NORMAL."

KinderMourn

When I finally returned to work on a part-time basis several weeks after the funeral, I was still in an eerie fog, which prevented me from concentrating on my work. I couldn't do the tasks I did before without feeling disconnected, as if this was all something I could not comprehend. I was still suffering from Post Traumatic Stress Disorder, which no one there could understand. Some people told me about losing their parents, which had nothing to do with what I was experiencing. It made me angry, although I knew they were only trying to relate somehow. But, it was not even remotely the same.

I lost my own father on New Year's Eve 1999. Yes, I was depressed for many months, but I had also watched him slowly dying for the past year and knew the end was coming. In addition, I knew on a conscious level that I would one day bury my parents. It was very difficult to see my dad die and lose the connection I had with him all of my life. I felt sad for my boys; Pete and Mike had loved their grandfather dearly and missed him so much. I was depressed for a long time as I grieved his loss.

But, this time I was suffering from grief and *trauma* – an unimaginable combination, one from which I feared I would never recover. I remember breaking into inconsolable crying, because I could not concentrate. I could not bear to be in a place where no one understood the pain, where no one understood the grief, where no one understood my resentment that others could go on with their lives when mine had changed unimaginably forever. I didn't know how to exist anymore. It's unexplainable to anyone who has not suffered the loss of a child, and yet I spent my days with people who hadn't a clue. I felt helpless, disoriented and defeated.

A colleague referred me to an organization called KinderMourn, a support group for bereaved parents. I was surprised to walk into a beautiful, warm, homelike atmosphere, with rooms embellished with comfy sofas and overstuffed cloth chairs. The welcoming first impression I received was much different than the stark, brightly lit room with metal folding chairs that I envisioned. The KinderMourn house radiated the loving, caring environment necessary for healing. I didn't say much on my first visit, but at the next meeting when I had to speak, much of the session consisted of my story and my uncontrollable tears. I found myself with other parents who had also lost their children under traumatic circumstances, just gone in a moment in time, which we could never regain. All of our children were young adults, between the ages of eighteen and thirty, and we all felt having them leave at such a young age had destroyed us. We missed the expectations we had for their lives – watching them grow into adulthood as parents themselves, being involved as grandparents one day, having family dinners and celebrations together and commemorating their accomplishments that were still to come. Our lives were changed forever, and we didn't know how to live in a "new normal."

Most of the credit for the healing in our group goes to two remarkable counselors, Elizabeth and Rich. They encouraged us to find whatever helped us to cope, whether it be psychics, commemorations, setting aside a specific time to grieve or reliving all our innumerable memories of our children. Sharing those memories brought us closer together and at times allowed us the release of laughter as we recalled some of the crazy things our kids did. One evening, a new member coming in thought she was in the wrong place because she heard laughter before she entered. Eventually, she too began to understand we could only do this within the meeting, because these were the only people who could understand that the laughter came through painful tears.

After my first few visits, I tried to resign because it was too painful for me. But Elizabeth understood what I was feeling. She called and talked with me and wouldn't let my excuses keep me away. I told her the meetings started too late, so she asked the members how they felt about starting earlier. They agreed to start an hour earlier for me. I told her I didn't feel I could share some of my seemingly off-the-wall feelings with others, yet she told me I needed to do just that, it could help others to see things in a different light. She had me. I realized she didn't let go of those in pain easily. She empathized and fought to help each and every one of us. Our group developed a real camaraderie and caring for each other. One member, Lisa, began to write poems to open and close the sessions, and those poems reflected how we all felt. We were all in the same place. We began to know each other's children and their stories. How different they all were, yet how very much the same they were to us as parents. We also felt our children knew each other now on the Other Side and were there with us in each session.

One evening, I brought the lyrics to a song by Matchbox 20 called *Unwell*. We all identified with the chorus to that song.

I'm not crazy I'm just a little unwell
I know right now you can't tell
But stay awhile and maybe then you'll see
A different side of me
I'm not crazy I'm just a little impaired
I know right now you don't care
But soon enough you're going to think of me
And how I used to be

The song epitomized where we were in time, and it became our theme song. I recall when a new member heard us talking about some of our signs from our deceased children as we were leaving. The woman looked at us as if we were crazy. Lisa assured her, "We're not crazy, we're just a little unwell." That said it all. Often it took awhile before some parents were open to the "coincidences" and signs from their children, but what an amazing meeting we had when someone started the meeting with, "Let me tell you what happened to me this week!"

The following October marked a year since I'd begun attending KinderMourn. I don't know what I would have done without their support. We began getting together for dinner before our sessions to talk amongst ourselves. That year Halloween fell on a Friday night. Two other moms and my "angel" friend, Helen, decided to join each other for a casual dinner and then go to Mike's cemetery since it was so private – an historic church cemetery located at the end of a dead-end street. We brought our children's urns and pictures with us and lit candles as we laid out our chaise lounges and ice chests of wine. That was the only place any one of us wanted to be. Although it was never discussed, I believe our plan was our escape from the festivities of costumed, neighborhood children bellowing "Trick or Treat." The memories of times we had once taken such pleasure in, as we participated with our own costumed children and their excitement for that special night, were just too hard to endure. I believe Helen was there to ensure I didn't fall off the deep end. We sat covered with blankets and talked about our children as if we were at a social event. No fear – fear never even occurred to us as we sat in the dark, deserted cemetery on that cool, fall night with candles at the end of a dead-end street. It was exhilarating.

At our next meeting, Mary brought the photos from Halloween night in the cemetery, beautiful pictures of our children's photos and urns on Mike's candle-lit grave under the tall, bare trees. There were orbs everywhere – we definitely spent the evening with several spirits. Even those who didn't believe were entranced and somewhat enthused by what they saw – maybe closer to belief. Our counselor, Elizabeth, surely did not make light of it. She explained to everyone what an orb was and how significant they were.

I attended KinderMourn for eighteen months and still support the organization with donations and often attend the emotional, annual memorial service in December. The ceremony takes place on a Sunday afternoon in a church, which generously donates this special time, and is always packed with bereaved parents and family members, each waiting their turn to walk down the aisle carrying a symbolic candle for their child. It's very emotional as I bear witness to the pain of other parents as they announce their child's name, give a short summation of their child's cause of death and the date. Each parent then places their candle alongside others on the two cloth-covered tables at the front of the church. The candles' glimmering radiance illuminate the church with a spirit-like glow. It's an overpowering experience.

But you always know when it's time to go. In fact, most of us decided to leave at about the same time. It was time to take what we learned together and live it. It was too difficult to keep reliving our children's stories each time a new member joined. Several of us commemorated our last month together with a weekend trip to the beach. It was tough – we all had needs for that farewell trip, but being together while we made the transition from unbearable grief to a mode of acceptance was another part of the journey. We still keep in touch and remember each other on holidays and anniversaries and will be forever grateful to each other for what we shared and for what we learned. I will also be forever grateful to Elizabeth and

Rich. They took me from the place of no return to the stage of finding my way.

Mystical Messages from Mike

Mike's friends dropped in on me often in those first few months after his death, and I could feel what I called the "Mikie energy" with us each time. Often it seemed as if Mike had sent them at a particular time, or for some specific reason. I recollect one melancholy day when I didn't want to get out of bed. The house was a mess and I hungered to lie there and not have to face another day of my horrendous nightmare. The phone rang and it was one of Mike's friends, "one of the guys."

"Hi, Ms. Ludman!" What are you doing? We want to come out to see you."

"Oh, that would be great! When do you want to stop over?" I asked.

"Tonight, about seven o'clock!" came the reply.

Oh my God! I was shaken from my despair and immediately went into overdrive. I had to clean up my act and get the house and myself together. As soon as I hung up the phone I knew Mikie was responsible. He didn't want me to wallow in my depression; he didn't want me to lose the fight. He was sending his crew to the rescue! It was just like him. I recall an incident that occurred when I was struggling with a statistics class. I was working full time and going to classes in the evening to finish my degree. I came home in tears one night convinced I couldn't handle the class; it was too hard! I definitely received a lesson from my son that night. Mike was a senior in high school. He just looked me in the eye and told me point blank, "You can't quit. What kind of example would that be for me?" And then he asked, "How bad do you want this, Mom?" Well, for the first time I realized it wasn't what I said to the boys, but how I was living. That was their example. Wow, what a revelation! Now, whenever I feel despondent or fall into that black hole, I hear Mike say, "What kind of example would that be for me?" At the time I had no concept of just how much influence those words would have on the rest of my life. And yes, I did finish the class and got a B!

The guys came to visit and the girls also came to spend time with me. One evening, Mike's friend Julie brought dinner and a beautiful silver locket engraved with Mike's name. Another time she presented me with the poem she had written for Mike, *Heaven's Calling,* and shared many of her memories of their friendship and dating relationship. Megan came quite often and would occasionally spend an entire afternoon with me. Once we visited Mike's accident site together. We would talk about Mike, cry about Mike and hold each other to console each other.

During those first few weeks, Mike's friend Amanda came to visit and asked for pictures of Mike. She was creating a collage for a design class at school. The finished project was breathtaking. She captured so much of Mike's essence on that canvas. I could tell how much their friendship meant to her. In the middle of the illustration was the very last photograph of Mike taken at brunch in Pensacola the weekend before his accident. He was sitting at the head of the long dinner table, with the bay glimmering through the full-length window in the background. Mike wore his well-known, irresistible grin and his deep, brown eyes appeared to see right into your soul. His thin beard and mustache and short, shaven brown hair framed his beautifully bronzed face; he did love the sun. Of course, Mike was dressed in a dark blue Nautica tee shirt with a short-sleeved over-shirt of white, deep blue and sky blue. The ensemble was completed with his infamous gold chain and necklace with the gold cross. The photo was the quintessence of Mikie.

Helen borrowed the canvas and had a copy made since I would soon have to return the original. I didn't know what she was up to until I walked in the house one evening and discovered a framed copy laying against a chair in my dining room. Now I would have it forever. Helen is the most caring, loving and thoughtful person I have ever known. She took the canvas to a print shop and was told by the technician it would never work – the canvas was too big and it would be too difficult, if even at all possible, to piece it together. But Helen has faith. She asked the technician if he believed in angels. His only response was to continue working with the canvas. He was amazed at the results. No one can tell it's pieced together. I didn't even know until Helen explained her encounter. Helen, "the faithful" made a believer out of the young man that day.

One night I had an extraordinary experience while asleep. No, it wasn't a dream; it was more of an insight or awareness. Briefly, a young woman's smiling face with long, straight brown hair flashed before my eyes. As I was jolted from my sleep, I felt the sensation of a strong friendship and a "knowing" that there was a connection to horses and Texas. It was so bizarre, yet amazing. I believe this must be the mode of communication for psychics. The first person I thought of was Mike's friend Amanda. She had light brown, straight hair and they had a very special friendship. But I didn't understand the connection to Texas. I called her the next day and asked if she had ever lived in Texas. "Yes, I spent some time there training horses," came her reply!

I knew, with an unexplainable knowing, I was supposed to go to Wilmington, where Mike had lived for most of the last year of his life. Amanda had attended school there and befriended Mike during that period. I told her about my middle of the night encounter and added that Mike said "hello." I'm not sure what she thought of that statement, but she agreed to meet me in Wilmington and show me the places where he spent so much of his time. Finally, I would have a chance to visit Mike, but alas, it would only be the memories of him.

We started at a little café called The Salt Works, where the kids used to hang out for a quick inexpensive meal and camaraderie. Then we headed to the stable where Amanda had worked part-time. She wanted me to ride the horse that Mike never had the chance or the opportunity to ride. I'm not sure if, perhaps, this was of his making; he was always a little cautious about new adventures. The owners were very understanding and allowed me to ride the show horse Mike was supposed to ride. It was fantastic. It was a delightful, sunny fall day with a Carolina Blue sky. As I rode the exquisite horse around the arena I felt such joy that I broke into laughter. All of a sudden I felt Mike's presence, so I talked to him and asked him if he was enjoying his ride. Oh, we definitely enjoyed our ride.

When we left the ranch, Amanda and I stopped at a convenience store to get water. I opened the refrigerator door and noticed one red rose in a basket in the cooler. I just knew I was supposed to purchase it as a gift for Amanda. When I got back in the car, I handed her the rose and told her it was from Mike. She seemed to understand. That was Mike's signature gift. Then I noticed the clock; it was 4:44 – the sign of the angels.

We continued on to Wrightsville Beach, where Amanda said Mike and his friends spent many sunset evenings and nights, just relaxing and shooting the breeze. We arrived at the perfect time at a spot where the boats drift in from the ocean to the harbor – a great place to appreciate the sun setting over the dunes across the inlet and the exact location where Mike and his friends would get together. We set our beach towels upon the cool sand and spent the most peaceful and mystical hour together with Mike. Oh, he was definitely there. There seemed to be a reverence engulfing the beach. Fishermen lingered patiently in an almost meditative state. Even the boaters appeared to appreciate the beauty and the serene setting as they shifted their motors to a nearly silent drift. The energy was powerful. Flocks of seagulls swooped down in front of us and back up to the heavens again. Two dolphins swam tranquilly from the harbor to the ocean. Amanda said that in the two years she lived there she had never once seen a dolphin. We shared this magical time as we viewed the most colorful, spirit-inspiring sunset I'd ever seen, which seemed to last forever. We gazed intently as the delicate blues, soft pinks, warm purples and striking oranges melted together and dissolved beyond the dunes across the harbor. We spoke in whispers so as not to disturb the tranquil atmosphere that felt so full of grace. It was hard to tear ourselves away as the sun disappeared and the darkness and cool breezes crept onto the beach.

There was one more place Amanda wanted to introduce me to before she had to head back to Charlotte. It was basically a fish camp nestled with other small seafood establishments along the harbor. Obviously a popular spot – we narrowly beat the long line of folks waiting for a seat. It was just perfect, a great little, inexpensive, seafood diner with fast service and good food. But it was also a jolt back to reality I wasn't quite ready for. I still wanted to hold on to the peace and sense of wonder, a sense of another dimension I experienced on the beach. Actually, I wished that feeling would stay with me for the rest of my days on this earth; but how do you hold on to something like that?

Amanda made sure I was settled into my bed and breakfast on Carolina Beach before she left. It was so sweet how she took charge. I had chosen this B&B because it was within walking distance of the Carolina Fishing Pier, where Mike and his friends Burt and Adam went to fish. Since it was early November, it wasn't surprising that I was the only guest. The innkeepers were very gracious and gave me their best room, which overlooked the rocking-chair porch and the ocean. What a gift! The same sensation I had experienced earlier on the beach returned as I heard the roar of the ocean. Waves tumbled, crashed and lapped at the shore right outside my bedroom.

I sat late into the evening rocking in the salt-water, musty rocker and writing in my Mikie journal on the quaint porch overlooking the ocean – nothing fancy, just typical beachy comfort. The owner came out to join me for a while and I told her about my day and the purpose of my visit. We then noticed, as more and more stars burst through the dark sky, that they only appeared in front of us above the ocean and over the house. She told me she had lived there for seven years and had never seen anything like it. She thought it was a sign from Mike. As she headed into the house for the night, she turned back and exclaimed, "You have an awesome son!"

Around noon on Saturday I walked along the beach to the Carolina Beach Fishing Pier. The blue-green ocean was calm and tranquil. There were surfers out past the break waiting patiently for the few "surfable" waves that would form from time to time. Several fishermen lined the surf waiting for a bite or exclaiming over their catch. As I walked the pier I noticed people of all ages, relaxed, laid back and in tune with nature, some even enjoying a beer. I passed two teenage boys chilling out and enjoying the sunshine as they awaited a tug on their line and I imagined what Mike and his buddies must have been like while fishing off this pier and unwinding with a beer. I could feel Mike walking beside me.

It was another clear, Carolina Blue day, so I found a spot by the railing to stand and enjoy the atmosphere and my surroundings. When I looked up at the sky, I noticed a cloud-like mass encircling the sun, maybe ten to twelve times larger than the sun. There were no other clouds in the sky. The outer edge of the formation was rimmed by all the colors of the rainbow. It was the most unusual thing I'd ever seen and the energy I felt was extraordinarily strong as I stared at the awe-inspiring sight for at least twenty minutes. I couldn't take my eyes off the sun. There was a pull and a power that was trancelike.

Eventually I pulled myself away and embarked on my walk down the beach to the B&B. I looked up to be sure the mysterious and mesmerizing rainbow cloud was still there. As I shielded my eyes from the bright noonday sun, it hit me. How could I have been staring at the sun? It was much too intense and glaring to even glance at. But I had stood staring at it for so long, with no problem, paralyzed by the mystical display! People on the pier must have thought I was very strange indeed. I had been involved in a miracle – a miracle of the sun, which I felt Mike gave me as a sign he was glad I was here.

Sunday morning was a breezy, cloudy day and everything seemed hushed in an atmosphere of solitude. I found myself walking and walking and I didn't really want to stop. Only the fishermen were out on the beach so early and even they seemed different today, very quiet and entranced. A very curious energy prevailed, almost melancholic. As I stood in the calm waves lapping the shore, I got the message. It's hard to explain – there are no voices in my head, but the thoughts are definitely not mine. Maybe it's a form of telepathy. I very clearly got

Mike's message, "Thanks for coming to see this part of me, Mom, but now go home and take care of my brother." That was how Mike often referred to Pete, as "my brother," even to relatives and friends.

Leaving Carolina Beach that afternoon, I crossed the bridge to the highway, put on a Marvin Gaye CD and said, "Okay Mike, let's go home." That became a pattern I followed each time I made my journey to Wilmington. I felt as if I rode with Mike.

When I returned home that evening, the first thing I did was pick up the phone and call Pete to tell him I was coming to Knoxville the next weekend. Mike was so right. I needed to be with Pete; we needed to be together, to hold each other up, to cry and to figure out how we would go on without our Mike.

My Visit to Knoxville

I left Charlotte on a delightful, crisp Friday afternoon and encountered another exceptional sunset as I drove through the mountains. It engulfed the whole heavens with oranges, reds, pinks and purples. There was no question in my mind – this was a present from Mike – extraordinary sunsets. The magnificent sight of amazing colors was painted across the late afternoon vista for most of the last hour of my trip. I couldn't take my eyes off the mesmerizing spectacle, which made for a somewhat difficult drive with cars whizzing past me at 85-miles-an-hour. But I realized I was heading in the right direction – Mike was guiding me to Pete. I knew I was doing what I was supposed to do and what Mike wanted me to do – I was going to take care of his brother.

As I drove, I thought about my first visit to see Pete in Knoxville after Mike's death. My friend Lesley had been staying with me and helping me. She took me to the police station for Mike's accident report; she wrote out my bills and handed them to me to sign, and she took care of the details as I tagged along in my trance-like daze. Les was not one I could talk to about all the pain I was going through, but she knew how to help me in other ways by taking care of me and getting me to Pete. She knew how important it was for me to be there with him. Pete doesn't share his grief easily with others. Josh, his roommate and good friend, was probably the only person he even talked to about Mike.

On that first trip, Lesley and her husband, Jim, drove me to Knoxville to be with Pete. We began as if it was just a typical visit, having friendly conversations with Pete and his roommates. It was a distraction to make things feel "normal" for a while. Then Pete, Josh and Mark took us down the block to Manhattan's, a neighborhood bar and restaurant. We had dinner and drinks and all went well until the conversation veered to Mike and stories of Peter and Mike. Then the dam broke. It wasn't long before Pete and I were both sobbing at the table with the rest of our group looking on quietly and helplessly. I had no idea what was going on around us in the standing room only bar. We were in full "Mikie grief mode." No one knew what to do. That was the way life went at that time – making people around us uncomfortable and feeling helpless to comfort us. They didn't understand the nightmare we lived each day and the pain that haunted us every waking moment.

Pete was still living in the "Old City," in a loft in the heart of all the bars and restaurants close to downtown Knoxville. He loved being a part of the inner city neighborhood and living near entertainment and work. When I arrived it was hard to explain to Pete the breathtaking and mysterious sunset that had guided me to him – it was really quite a phenomenon, even more impressive than the sunset on Wrightsville Beach. It wasn't until his buddy Josh walked into the apartment and exclaimed, "Ms. Ludman, did you see that unbelievable sunset?" that Pete realized it wasn't just his crazy mom – there was something remarkable from Mike that he missed. He was beginning to understand and also becoming aware of another dimension, which his life now included.

We began our visit as usual – evading the subject of Mike. After dinner in the Old City we planned a day of hiking in the mountains the next day. Plans changed as a cool, rainy day greeted us Saturday morning. A little thing like the weather no longer had any importance – it was just the idea of being together. So Pete and I set off for Gatlinburg with our rain gear. We had lunch at a quaint German restaurant, shopped for a while and then visited the Aquarium. It was another prolonged distraction as we casually moseyed through and let go of time, and just went with the flow. We ended up at each feeding area exactly when the staff was explaining the types of fish in that specific tank and had front row seats as the diver fed the aquatic animals. As we continued to the end of the tour, we discovered a pool filled with stingrays. Visitors were allowed to pet the stingrays, stinger removed, and Pete and I joined with the others. After an indoor game of putt-putt, there were no more reasons for distractions and we headed back to Knoxville for dinner. The subject we had been avoiding was now our main focus – Mike.

We talked about many things that evening and shared many memories, some of which I never knew, things that were between Pete and Mike. Some things I knew I would probably never know. As our eyes began to tear we headed back to the hotel. The raging storm within us was now out in the open. Pete told me that Mike was the reason he gets out of bed each morning, but Mike was also the reason he didn't want to get out of bed each morning. So much turmoil, conflict and grief engulfed us as we sat in my hotel room. Pete sobbed – an awful cry of pain and anguish. We held each other and rocked back and forth until we were cried out. This is how our visits went for the next few years. First came the avoidance and then we could no longer pass the time in denial – we needed to comfort each other, but we had yet to learn how to move forward and accept that Mike was gone. It took many years before each of us could begin that journey.

It was so hard leaving Pete that Sunday afternoon, but I knew I couldn't stay with him. He had his life in Knoxville and lived with roommates, so we could only help each other over the phone and during the short times we were together. Life shouldn't be that way. But alas, society doesn't recognize or acknowledge the overwhelming pain and grief that other cultures allow. We had to try to be "normal."

As hard as we tried, those times of sharing and comforting each other disrupted many occasions. Even family members felt powerless and anxious around us, especially as we encountered the holiday season and the "first of the firsts." We tried our best to escape the festive atmosphere of the season, but we had no choice as we were surrounded by a raging whirlwind of gloom.

I think back to our first Thanksgiving without Mike. My mom and my sister, Theresa, came from New Orleans to visit, offer comfort and share in our grief. Images were brought to mind as I prepared the turkey, sweet potato casserole and Mike's favorite, macaroni and cheese. I was busy in the kitchen until I observed Pete sitting quietly at the dinner table gazing sadly at the backyard. I felt he was picturing himself throwing the football with Mike – just the way things used to be. Mike was expected to be here. I envisioned them laughing and wrestling in the living room as they often did. I stopped what I was doing and went to Pete. As I hugged him, he broke down with a gut-wrenching cry. My mother and sister left us alone. The food could wait. It was now just a meaningless ritual. When we finally sat down to Thanksgiving dinner, Pete looked up with tear-stained eyes and lashed out – "No pictures, no saying grace and no giving thanks!" We all understood and I believe we all knew that was to be avoided as we ate mostly in silence. This was no longer an enjoyable family holiday. It was now a day of painful memories as we took our seats around the dinner table with the empty chair.

The anguish and despondency were even worse at Christmas. Pete and I met in New Orleans and stayed with my brother, Chip, my niece, Katie and my four-month-old great nephew, Dominic. It should have been a joyful time, celebrating baby's first Christmas. Instead, there was an intense cloud of sadness that hung heavily in the air, especially on Christmas Eve. I couldn't fight the anxiety that rose within me as Pete and I walked into my mother's house for the annual opening of Christmas gifts. Immediately, I sensed the apprehension and concern of my family as they anticipated our struggle to be "normal." As I scanned the room full of family pictures and collages, I wept uncontrollably. Pete hugged me and took me out to the front porch. He held me tightly in his arms in the cold, damp night air as I sobbed. It was as if I was in Mike's arms. I was very grateful to my family for that time alone with Pete. That's what we did. It seemed we always put on the usual pretense until we were alone together and could finally let down our guard.

This is what our lives had become – feelings of denial, anger, pain and grief, but as of yet, no acceptance. That was still beyond our comprehension. That would be a long time to come.

A Reading for "The Boys"

Shortly after my first private session with psychic-medium Mary Beth Wrenn, Mike's friends came for another visit. As the night went on, I finally shared my experience with them. I said Mary Beth was very sure a man's hands were on the steering wheel when the accident happened, but I explained that Nick's girlfriend was driving. Nick's eyes began to tear as he described those last moments. He said the car was spinning out of control on the wet road, so he grabbed the wheel to go into the direction of the spin as he had been taught. That news dumbfounded us. The guys asked if they could make an appointment with Mary Beth too. I agreed to set up a reading for them, but wanted to know when they could all attend. The answer was, "The first available!"

Mike's buddies and I had our meeting the Saturday before Mike's burial of ashes and memorial service. Adam,

Sean, Josh, Lou, Nick, Nelson and Chris were all there and very excited, yet anxious and skeptical as we entered Mary Beth's house. We were all seated around the living room, some on the floor. Then Mike joined us. His personality was so unlike he was with me. Now he was with his friends and I could see how distinctive his relationship was with them – a very different energy and attitude. Mike and the guys had a unique bond I hadn't been privy to in this special friendship they shared. The day was memorable because the boys related their own stories of Mike's visits to them, and Mary Beth revealed so much that was on target and also had profound meaning for them. This is what I wrote in my journal about that day:

Saturday, December 7, 2002

Well, Lovebug, you were in rare form today. It was so important to the guys that you were there for them and were able to tell them the things you did. You have changed their lives forever. You gave them validation that you live on and are still with them.

I know it was significant to Adam when you talked about the strong bond between the two of you. Mary Beth asked if you were brothers. Megan had just given me a photo to give to Adam of the two of you on a camping trip. She had the picture bordered in a frame titled, "Other Brothers." Mary Beth saw a purple energy around Adam and kept referring to that strong bond between you both. She told him he had been to the cemetery where your ashes will be buried many times before. Adam didn't remember until later how he had played in the cemetery often when he was young. Sean didn't know what to make of the writing thing you talked about, he doesn't think of himself as a writer, yet that is what you asked of him. He may have understood a little more when you alluded to his deep, sensitive nature and thoughts. (Of course, the boys ragged on him about that.) Mary Beth repeatedly saw a blue energy around Sean and told him you wanted him to write about you. (Sean did write a beautiful story for me a few months later, which I cherish.)

Mary Beth then asked about the Michelin Man (or what she thought was the Michelin Man). As she previously explained, she can only go by her own frame of reference when she is shown visions from the Other Side. No one understood until after the session when Adam showed her the tattoo over his heart of a cross with your name and dates and Sean showed her his tattoo on his shoulder of a cross with the "Big Worm" (your nickname) wrapped around it. "That's it!" Mary Beth exclaimed. "That's the Michelin Man Mike was showing me, but I didn't know how to explain it!" I believe you had a message for Sean but it was lost because she didn't understand what it was she saw. Or maybe you were only acknowledging the tattoo and letting Sean know it pleased you.

During the session, Mary Beth stated that you had appeared to either Adam or Sean as an illusion, but they weren't really sure if it was you. They are now. Sean's already told me something to that effect. It's definitely made an impression on them. All of the guys have since told me stories of you "messing" with them, as they put it.

You blew Nick away with your messages about him when he and his family were on vacation soon after the accident. You described an A-frame structure and a very large deck. Nick was in tears by this time and he later told me he and his family had gone to Cancun for vacation and there was a very large deck where all the activities were held. You also brought in his cousin Tony, who died years before on his twenty-first birthday and had messages for his mom, Nick's aunt. Nick knew you were with him. Then you mentioned a screen door and tools and said you would be messing with their tools. I didn't know until that moment that you and Nick and Josh were talking about starting a remodeling business and you would be handling the plumbing work. Mary Beth told them you were really excited about the remodeling business and if they were ever missing tools to ask you to give them back. That brought a laugh and everyone agreed it certainly sounded like you.

Mary Beth then turned to Nelson and referred to the pyramid she saw over his head, which symbolized his psychic energy. It turned out Nelson had been reading up on the afterlife and was meditating before he went to sleep so he could communicate with you in his dreams. He stated he actually does connect with you. He added that he paid attention previously when I told him you were a Dream Rescuer (this I had been told in a private session).

She told Lou he was the life of the party, the center of attention and a quick wit with quick comebacks. All the guys laughed and affirmed that was definitely Lou. Chris was recognized as a very old soul and there was a spirit trying to make contact with him, but he couldn't identify the person.

At one point, you showed Mary Beth a vision of the Rolling Stones symbol with the long tongue hanging out, but no one would admit to a connection. She finally pointed to Nick and exclaimed, "It was you!" Nick starting laughing through his tears and she asked if he understood. He responded he did, but he wasn't going to talk about it in front of Mike's mom.

Well, Mike, you were certainly being yourself and playing with them, but they loved it and knew for sure you were there with them. You gave validation to all the times you've been "messing" with them.

You also told Mary Beth you hold no grudges and for some reason that seemed to be important to some of the guys. She said you wanted everyone to move forward and get on with life. She also got the impression you were not very interested in the memorial we have planned for next weekend, but Mike, you have to understand that the memorial is for us, the living. We need to do what we need to do on this side.

The last thing you mentioned (as you did in a previous session) was that you wanted me to ride horses and go dancing again. And then you were gone, although we still had so many questions left to ask. A teasing comment was made about me and Mary Beth responded, "It's like Mike said, 'That's my momma!'" Oh, how many times have I heard that in the last few months? When I did something a little off the wall, you would always tell your friends, "That's my momma, you gotta love

91

her!" The boys shared with me how you often said that when I did something to embarrass you, like the night I howled at the moon with my friends. I do believe I probably embarrassed you and Pete in your teenage years a lot more than I realized. Payback!

It was funny when we left Mary Beth's house. The guys had come in two cars and she gave us a tape of the session. They were arguing that no one could listen to the tape until they were all together at Chris' house. It was endearing to me. You may be gone, Mike, but the group is still the same, brothers to the end, bickering over such things. But that's who you all are. It was such a privilege for me to see you in the company of the boys – so different than when you communicated with me. That's what makes it real and accurate, the change in personality – one way with the guys and another with me. I felt honored to see that relationship and the laughter and bond you shared with your family of friends.

I believe we left that day knowing any doubts we may have had about communication with Mike on the Other Side were gone – Mike was still with us and connecting in different ways. We were all beginning to understand our connection to, and the reality of, the Other Side. Mike is just in another dimension, and he will always be with the guys and with all those who knew and loved him.

The Memorial and Burial of Ashes

Shortly after Mike's funeral, or maybe it was at the funeral (I remember so little about that), one of the boys expressed concern about our decision to have Mike cremated. They would have no special place to go and be with him. The idea of Mike being completely gone from our lives was inconceivable. I realized we had to find a cemetery where we could bury some of Mike's ashes. In the next week, while Pete was still in town, he and Ed and I went to a few cemeteries to begin looking. It was all so impersonal, so cold and business-like. We actually drove over burial plots in a golf cart with a salesperson at one cemetery. This was too much. It was also too much for Ed to handle; he insisted he had to get away from there.

As we headed to another cemetery located closer to Mike's old neighborhood (we all wanted Mike to be near where he grew up and spent so much time with his friends), I remembered a quaint little cemetery where a friend of mine was buried. Mike had attended the funeral with me and held me close as I cried. So we set out to the Matthews Historical Cemetery. It was a small, old cemetery maintained by a nearby church, which was nestled sweetly at the end of a dead-end street under huge shade trees, which allowed for privacy. Compared to the restrictions of the others we had seen, there were pretty much no "rules" here. Mike would like that. We found the perfect site near the cemetery's edge, under the trees and at the entrance to a lovely meditation garden. It was settled. This would be Mike's resting place, a place where anyone could visit at any time, day or night.

A few weeks later Lesley came to spend several days with me and take care of the empty shell of a person I had become. She took me to the funeral home to purchase the grave for Mike's ashes. While we were there, the funeral director gave me information about a woman who had lost her son a few years earlier and now worked with other bereaved parents to design their children's headstones. That in itself was a gift. Again Les took charge, made an appointment and then took me to see this special lady. As we entered her office Les gave me a "thumbs-up." The room was filled with Native American art. There were mandellas, dream-catchers, other Native American paintings and figurines. Les knew how much I was in sync with the Native American culture and had been since my college years. I have so many of the same items in my own home, including a mandella on the wall above my bed. It is believed by Native Americans to bring health, happiness and prosperity, along with prayers for survival, spiritual blessings and powerful visions. We trusted it was a sign, and we were so right. This incredible woman, whom I'll refer to as Jean, was so kind, caring and personal. She helped me select a beautiful and fitting headstone for Mike and was in touch often as we completed design details. Before we left her house, she asked if she could pray with me. Oh, this was such a completely different experience than I had encountered at other companies. I realized Jean did what she did out of love, because she had been through the same heartache when she lost her son and she definitely made sure other parents would have a better experience when burying their children.

Now it was up to Pete, Ed and me to decide on the inscription for Mike's headstone. After many faxes back and forth we decided on his full name, his dates and a short verse. His headstone was simple, yet strong and personal. The inscription read:

Michael Edward Ludman
April 30, 1980 – August 17, 2002
"A generous soul, with a big heart and beautiful smile.
He touched the lives of so many"

On the day I met Jean at the cemetery to finalize the dimensions and epitaph for Mike's headstone, she shared with me that her son died on Mike's birthday – another coincidence which no longer surprised me. As I left the cemetery in tears, I asked Mike to give me a sign he was okay with the headstone and our plans for the memorial service when it was in place. I stopped at the grocery to pick up a few things, still doing things in a stupor. As I walked out of the store there was a man collecting for a charity. He told me excitedly, "Look at the double rainbow!" I glanced up and saw such an amazing sight, a magnificent double rainbow arching across the cloudy sky, a sight not seen very often, if at all. I loaded my groceries and proceeded to the exit for home. While sitting at a red light, the woman in the next car rolled down her window and motioned to me. I thought I must have a flat tire or something. So I rolled down the window and she pointed and said, "Look at the double rainbow!" How weird, I thought, for this woman to do this. I smiled and responded they were glorious and rare. I then drove home in tears. It wasn't until I was writing in my Mikie journal in the evening that I laughed and realized Mike did indeed send me a sign, an incredible gift, a double rainbow. That was my first double rainbow from Mike, but it wasn't my last.

Mike was always giving me gifts. He derived much joy from giving and making others happy, but he also liked the acknowledgement. He would always have that from me. I felt such sorrow for the parents who couldn't recognize and cherish those signs from their children. But, in the time I spent in KinderMourn, I saw many of the unbelievers turn into believers as they began to identify the signs which were so meaningful and appropriate for them. I shared in the joy and the comfort those connections brought to each and every one of them. We all realized this was our new way of communicating with our children and knew they were not lost, just in another dimension, which we were just beginning to understand.

When I shared the double rainbow event with my KinderMourn group, a few were skeptical, but most, including our counselors, were in awe of such a wonderful sign. A few months later, as we sat in our group, someone noticed a double rainbow in the late afternoon sky. We all crowded around the window and laughed as we claimed it as our own personal manifestation from our child. We all believed. We didn't know Lisa had run out to her car and captured a photo of the extraordinary double rainbow. The next week she arrived with an impressive, significant poem she had written, along with a copy of the photo for everyone in the group. What a treasure she was to all of us.

In the weeks before the memorial service, I had many dreams and awarenesses. I awoke from one dream with a "knowing." Mike told me I would recognize his presence through glitter, snowflakes and the wind. I asked him to let Pete know he was with him when Pete came home for the memorial and burial service. On that morning, Pete was awakened when Mike's alarm went off in his bedroom across the hall. It was exactly the time Mike would have gotten up for work. The clock radio was blaring the song, *The Future's So Bright, I Gotta Wear Shades,* by Timbuk3. Mike certainly does things in a big way. It startled and upset Pete and he hasn't slept in his bedroom since that night. Now when he comes to visit he sleeps on the sofa. But strangely enough, on another visit home, Pete experienced a "Mikie visit" before falling asleep on the living room sofa.

The headstone arrived in early December and we set the ceremony for December 14th. Mike's close friends were invited to the cemetery where we would dig a grave for the small, blue marble urn that held some of his ashes. More of Mike's ashes would be spread on Wrightsville Beach and off the Carolina Fishing Pier on his first anniversary. Most would stay with me in another blue urn, which would sit on my shelf forever. It had to be blue, Mike's favorite color.

As an unbelievably strong wind blew through the cemetery, Pete, and then each of Mike's friends, took turns digging with Mike's shovel, the one he used to dig so many of my gardens. You could see the anger in each face as the shovel slammed into the hard red clay over and over again. Helen read a prayer she'd written at my request. It was very spiritual and in tune with Mike, even though it was hard to understand the words through her tears and over the sound of the wind. I read the eulogy.

My Dearest Mikie,

There's a song by Sarah McLachlan I relate to since you left. She says, "Hold on. Hold on to yourself, for this is gonna hurt like hell." And it does. I miss you so much. I miss your smile as you walk in the door; I miss teasing you about 'that look' when you frown; I miss seeing you walk around with the telephone to your ear; I miss your strong, comforting hugs; I miss seeing you and Pete throwing the football out in the yard; I miss hearing your laugh; I miss hearing you talk about "my brother," I miss my son. Lovebug, it does hurt like hell.

From the time you were born, you were full of life and had so much energy. It was hard to keep up with you. We walked many paths together from those years so long ago to where you are today. Love, caring and respect have always been our bond, keeping us close even when we were apart. You have given me many gifts on our journey, but none more precious than the smiles you bring to my heart.

Through the years, I saw a gentle, sensitive, loving person who met many challenges and, at times, struggled to find his way. I could see you were finally finding your way, you were content with your life, you were proud of who you were, and you took great pride in a profession you came to love. I was hoping to see you enjoy that life with your own family. You would have been a terrific father with your sensitivity and depth, yet so childlike yourself. I will miss seeing all those little Mikies growing up. I would have spoiled them and sent them home, howling at the moon. You would have protested some, but then I see you shaking your head, smiling and saying, "That's my Momma!"

You shared your love and specialness with many people. You touched the lives of so many and truly made a difference. You made a lasting impression on this world; you gave something precious to me and many others. You touched my heart and my life in a way that has changed me forever.

Thank you for coming into my life and for allowing me the chance to learn and grow with you. I love you. I'm very proud of you. Until we are together again, I hold you in my heart and I smile and say "hello" when I feel you close to me, when I feel you in my heart, when I feel you watching over me. I love you, Mikie. Until we meet again.

Love,
Mom

Then Pete lovingly placed Mike's ashes in his resting spot. Mike's friend Julie read a poem she had written called *Heavens Waiting* and I laid a red rose on the grave. It was a very difficult and emotional day. I knew Mike was there because of the amazingly strong, cold wind gusting throughout the ceremony. Later, Amanda told me that as she stood with the wind blowing through her hair, she looked up and smiled, knowing Mike was the wind. I think somehow we all knew.

We ended the day at Megan's house. I brought several bottles of Remi Martin brandy, Mike's favorite, I was informed. As I talked with his friends they shared their many stories about Mike. There was one young man I had never met, but he seemed to love Mike and appreciate the fact that Mike was his friend. Pete told me Mike would always branch out from the main group of guys while at parties and out having fun. He made friends with everyone. Pete shared most people feared Mike because of his tough guy facade. But, he added, once they got to know him, they were his friends forever. I was still learning a lot about my son. Several people told me Mike always took up for the underdog. He wouldn't let others make fun of anyone not with the "in" group or anyone hindered in some way. I already knew that about my son, but didn't realize he was admired by his peers because of it. As his buddy Nelson put it, "Everyone respected Mike because Mike never disrespected anyone." Mike was still making me proud.

When it came time for Mike's toast I was instructed to pour a glass for him and told we had to go outside. As we raised our glasses, Adam held Mike's glass and poured his shot on the ground, as did many others. I discovered it was a tradition, as I was told about the party at Chris' house the weekend of Mike's funeral. The boys informed me there was so much beer poured on the ground in Chris' backyard, as they toasted Mike over and over again, that there was more beer soaking the yard than was consumed by all present. He would have liked that and I'm sure he was smiling and laughing his good-humored, mischievous laugh.

A few weeks later Helen met me for lunch with a very special surprise. She had stayed behind at the cemetery for a while to be with Mike after the memorial. She took two pictures from the same location of Mike's grave. Over his headstone, amongst the trees and the meditation garden, was a rainbow! Not a rainbow up in the sky, but a rainbow suspended above his grave, which now held his ashes. I've read that rainbows are God's heavenly stamp of approval. I believe this was Mike's smile of approval and his stamp on my heart.

Nature's Rainbows

We held them in our parent arms
For days or weeks or years.
Now we hold them in our hearts
And cry the darkest tears.

The cord attached to children,
Eternally fine and strong.
We never leave the missing,
It holds us all life long.

Our children now inside us –
Our souls tattooed with gold.
Their love, their words, caresses,
And hugs that we still hold.

If we open to the knowledge,
That they aren't completely gone,
We will sometimes feel their touching,
Sometimes soft and sometimes strong.

When they show us nature's rainbows,
We can feel their proud delight,
Sending signs to show they're living,
Only far beyond our sight.

By Lisa Roark

The Cemetery

After we buried Mike's ashes, I began to spend many of my days at the cemetery; I was constantly drawn there. It was an obsession. It was the only place I wanted to be. Often times, I'd leave work and spend an hour here and there, but especially on the weekends I was always there with Mike. It was important to me to have a fresh red rose on his grave at all times. Everyone who knew him would understand – a red rose was Mike's signature. At times, I'd sit on the little stool he and Megan had constructed from some scraps of sheetrock and write in my Mikie journal. Other days, I'd just sit and talk to him for an hour or so and sob. It was so out of my realm of comprehension. The cemetery was my special place to just "be" with Mike and I now understood why it had been so important to his friends to have a place to come to. No matter the temperature or the time of year, I sit with Mike. Sometimes it was so cold and barren, like my heart.

There were many experiences and signs that brought me comfort at the cemetery. On one visit I found Mike's grave covered in carefully arranged pine needles. It was extraordinary. I knew those needles were positioned ceremoniously by Helen. She and Mike had a special connection. Later Helen told me while sitting at home reading she felt Mike was calling her to the cemetery. She didn't understand why, but she knew she didn't have much of a choice. Mike could be very demanding at times and didn't like his requests to be ignored. Helen was very intuitive – she always just "knew." As if in a trance, she began gathering pine needles from the trees behind Mike's grave. We believed that we had all known each other in another lifetime. When she arrived at the cemetery, she asked him what she was supposed to do and she realized she was involved in a ritual, an Indian burial ritual. She heard his name, but could only remember the last part – "Hawk."

Helen often met me at the cemetery when I hadn't even told her I was going to visit Mike. But there she was, as if she knew. I believe for quite some time Helen was always there to watch over me to insure I didn't fall off the deep end, to be lost forever, never to recover. Soon after my discovery, while we were admiring Mike's ceremonial grave, a hawk flew just above us, circling and swooping as if playing and toying with us. Or maybe it was an acknowledgment and a thank you. Before long, another hawk joined the first; they playfully soared above us, then headed off in the direction of our old neighborhood. I will never forget my feeling of awe and joy as I laughed and cried while watching the hawks fly away. I had just been to the funeral of Mike's good friend Travis, who had also died in an auto accident. It was only eight months after Mike's accident and once again Mike's "family of friends" stood in disbelief at another gravesite, wondering what these tragedies were all about and who would be next. I believed the second hawk was Travis and he and Mike had found each other on the Other Side as they soared together through the clear blue sky.

During my next visit with Mary Beth, she described another person who was trying to connect. After she explained how he appeared to her, I immediately knew it was Travis. She depicted him as a young, blonde male, gasping to breathe, as if he was suffocating. In fact, that is exactly how Travis died – his chest was crushed when the car he'd been thrown from rolled on top of him. The guys had given Mike and Travis a twenty-first birthday party the year before because their birthdays were only one day apart. After Travis died his mother told me that Travis repeatedly said he would never make it to twenty-three. The number twenty-three again! Travis also told another friend, Julie, that he would soon be with Mike and they both would be "messing" with her. They certainly did. They sent different signs, caused pictures to fall off the wall and music to play when she hadn't turned on the stereo. As I've said before, somehow I think we know – on another level – when it's our time.

On Mike's first birthday Megan and I were planting a garden on his grave. Naturally, Megan planted two small, beautiful rose bushes close to Mike's headstone. Now she was giving back to him all the roses he had given to her during their years together. We had bags of gardening tools, soil, plants and mulch and we began to dig in the hard, red clay. After much frustration I exclaimed, "Where are the boys when you need them?" It wasn't but five minutes later that two of Mike's friends pulled up with bottles of Icehouse! They walked up smiling and said, "Hi Ms. Ludman. We just came out to have a beer with Mike." I'm sure that made Mike very happy. Well, in no time the guys were digging, working with Megan and me as we all shared their beer, then poured some on Mike's grave when we finished. Mike's is the only grave in the private, small historic cemetery with a garden and wind chimes. You can tell how much he was, and still is, loved.

I heard the guys went out to the cemetery late at night to drink beer and visit with Mike. I once asked if anyone smoked Marlboro Lights. They looked a little apprehensive and wanted to know why. I told them I found one near Mike's headstone. Finally Adam admitted it was his. He thought I was upset because he left the butt near Mike's grave. But when I explained I just wanted to make sure Mike wasn't still smoking on the Other Side, that brought a laugh from all the guys and a sigh of relief from Adam. They were glad to know I wasn't upset with them, but pleased that they went out to visit Mike and have a beer like old times. I know all this may sound strange, coming from a mother, but unless you've been there and experienced the pain and the loss, you don't understand the things that can bring you joy. You enjoy hearing about the way your child and his friends spent time together and feel comforted to know they still love and respect that friendship.

I never know when I will find new potted plants placed on Mike's grave by his friend Stacey. I try to ensure the new foliage is planted in time to take root and grow within the garden. She often brings her twin girls to visit the "angel" and they each bring a plant and balloon they've chosen. The cards Stacey leaves for Mike are always placed in his memory box. Stacey told me Mike would be there to listen to her when she needed a comforting shoulder to cry on, but he was also always the one who made her laugh and look at the bright side. Mike was the one who encouraged her to go back to school, which she did. She completed her degree just a few weeks before Mike's accident, but didn't have the opportunity to tell him the news. Pete told me she and Mike had a very special relationship and even had nicknames for each other.

I still go to the cemetery often and keep gardening tools and watering bottles in the trunk of my car, because sometimes I never know when I'll stop by. When I plan to visit, I prepare to make sure I have everything I need to clean his headstone and make his area tranquil, beautiful and cared for. It's the only real, physical thing I can do for my Mikie now. I feel peaceful as I spruce up the garden, especially when I hear the wind chimes. Often when I'm there I will hear the church bells ring from the nearby church. It's become known amongst my friends and Mike's that I will always be there on his birthday and on each anniversary. I bring red roses and make Mike's grave special in some way. Especially on his anniversary, friends will come out and sit with me. We'll have some wine or beer to toast Mike and stay until the garden night-lights come on. Now, each year on Mike's birthday and anniversary I bring a cold bottle of Icehouse (his favorite) and toast him as I pour the beer on his grave. A friend of Mike's (another Megan) was with me on his last anniversary. She poured about a third of the beer as we toasted and she questioned if that was enough. I asked if she thought Mike would say it was enough. She just laughed and emptied the rest of the bottle. We all knew Mike very well. The tradition would continue.

The first years were the hardest. I always had to take the day off from work, then after being at the cemetery with Mike, I'd come home a total wreck, drink too much and cry myself to sleep. But as the years pass, I do better at the cemetery and I do better when I get home, although I still take the day off from work. I just can't write that date over and over again while doing my job. There's also another reason for my perspective now, which is very sad, and not what I could ever have imagined for Megan or her parents. She was my special link to Mike. Megan is with him now. She was killed two years later and was buried close to Mike. Her dad and I care for both graves. Whenever I plant new plants or add something special, I do it for both Mike and Megan. So does her dad. I can always tell he's been there when I see new plants or bulbs blooming. Mike and Megan are together for all eternity. It's not how any of us envisioned their future, yet so many believed they would always be together.

A short time after Megan's death, as I was working on their gardens, I felt a presence in the woods behind their graves. I could feel laughter and joy. I felt as if they were playing amongst the trees, being so childlike and innocent. I grieve for them both. I had so many expectations of their life together as a family with their children. Now I know

I have to accept that they are not with us the way I always envisioned, but try to accept they're together in a paradise that I believe has brought them joy, peace and love beyond all comprehension.

The Game

How do you commemorate the "first" birthday of your son when he's not here to celebrate with you – the first birthday after you sat by his side and watched him die? It couldn't actually be a celebration, but I had to find a way to honor my son, a tribute that would make him proud and bring those who loved him together to acknowledge his short time on this side with us. The answer was *The Mike Ludman Memorial Softball Game.*

The idea originated when Amanda asked, "How are we going to celebrate Mike's birthday?" Birthdays were very important to him. I replied, as if someone put the words in my mouth, "We'll have a baseball game on his birthday!" One thing lead to another; everyone came up with ideas, and then it was official - "The Game," with Mike's "family of friends," their families, my family and all our dear friends who supported Pete and me through the most difficult of times. It was to become the only way I could make it through such an arduous and heart-wrenching time. We would charge admission, with the proceeds to benefit *A Child's Place,* a non-profit organization that helped homeless children. Mike would love that. He loved kids and could be such a kid himself.

It was time consuming and a lot of hard work, yet very distracting – during the planning stage I was so busy, I could no longer spend all my time grieving Mike's death. Megan helped me compile an invitation list and introduced ideas that I hadn't considered. Pete created the invitation. Of course, he chose his favorite picture of Mike for the cover. I selected the field and park shelter and worked on the reservation to ensure it occurred on the weekend before his birthday. I had banners printed; one read, *"Happy Birthday Mike"* and the other made the reason plain, *"The Mike Ludman Memorial Softball Game."* This was achieved with the help of a compassionate business owner and the assistance of my sister, Theresa, and my friend, Helen.

Everything came together, and "The Game" was a rousing success. It seemed to make a real difference to all those who knew and loved Mike. Love and laughter prevailed, instead of sadness and tears. I brought dozens of blue balloons so everyone could write messages to Mike, and then I released them to signify the beginning of the game.

The day was hot and humid and when the rain came, it didn't seem to put a damper on anyone's spirit. In fact, it appeared that the rain was a bonus. The boys loved sliding around in the mud, and there were so many comical and memorable moments on the field that afternoon. Players were covered in red clay instead of neat team jerseys. Most wore the official "Big Worm" T-shirts, made in loving memory of Mike by his close friend Sean, one of *The Weethees* (a name they called themselves). I therefore felt it fitting to name the teams *The Big Worms* and *The Weethees*.

Megan contributed a sheet cake with pictures of Mike in a baseball collage she had created scanned onto the top. We had "Mikie's Dip" – his favorite taco dip with chips. Aunt T brought wallet size photos, lovingly referred to as "Mike's Essence," to give to everyone attending. It was a perfect picture, which depicted the real spirit of Mike. My friends saw to the details as I mingled with Mike's buddies, played third base, talked with parents and took photos. As the game ended I realized everyone still wanted to linger and socialize. So I thought, "Next year we need a picnic!" The invitations, the banners, the balloons, the birthday cake, "Mikie's Dip" and "Mike's Essence" – were all to become traditions for *The Mike Ludman Memorial Game* in the years to follow.

On Mike's actual birthday, Pete was back in Knoxville, and I was planting a garden with Megan at the cemetery. When we said our good-byes I got in the car, and noticed a message from Pete on my cell phone. When I heard it, I laughed and I cried. Pete was so excited and amazed at the same time. He kept saying, "Oh my God, oh my God! A blue balloon, one frigging blue balloon! Oh my God!"

When I returned Pete's phone call he was still flabbergasted. He had tried to work that day, but found himself unable to concentrate. He decided to take Mike's golf clubs, which are now very special to him, and go to the driving range to let off steam and honor Mike at the same time. They had enjoyed many wild and crazy golf games together. Pete said that as he was hitting the balls, one blue balloon came floating out of nowhere, just one balloon with a string attached, which flew right over his head. He knew it was Mike saying, "Hi, big brother. Thanks for coming to spend time with me the way we used to." Pete had had other unusual experiences and had tried to explain them away in a rational way, but now he could no longer deny the obvious.

For the following year, a picnic was planned and another tradition began. The cake was an integral part of the celebration with a new picture scanned onto the top as we observed Mike's birthday with song and candles. Patrice, a childhood friend of mine from New Orleans, suggested we incorporate a different picture on the invitation each year so people would look forward to another special aspect of Mike. Pete liked the idea and I would await his e-mail once he had selected a favorite photo and sent it to me for approval. But no approval was necessary – that was Pete's job, to create the invitations. And it always warmed my heart when I saw the finished result. I wrote the details and dedicated "The Game" to an individual or individuals who were part of Mike's life.

Another concept was added to "The Game" that year as Ron Dion (known as Mr. D) and Bill Focht took over the roles of coaches for each team. They were Mike's coaches during league ball, the fathers of several of his close buddies and still very much a part of Mike's life at the time of his accident. Bill decided to award a trophy each year for *The Most Valuable Play* (note: not the most valuable player). He felt all the players were valuable and essential to the game, therefore he elected to recognize

The Most Valuable (or outstanding) Play. He also surprised us all with a lovely plaque to recognize the reason for the game – *The Mike Ludman Memorial Softball Game,* with nameplates for the winning teams for twenty-four years. Bill became the coach for *The Weethees* and more or less supervised play. Ron took the role of *The Big Worms'* coach. He also volunteered to cook the hamburgers and hot dogs for the picnic. As he slaved over hot coals, the participants eagerly awaited the barbecued hamburgers, played cards and socialized.

Mike's good friend, Nick, was paralyzed in a skiing accident just five months after Mike's accident. A foundation had been created to assist with his equipment and needs. The game now had a second beneficiary, *The Nick Focht Foundation.* Mike would have definitely approved. We also included *KinderMourn* as a recipient of the proceeds. The groundwork for the yearly event was laid. The game was a fundraiser for worthy causes that had a special significance to us, as well as an event to celebrate Mike's life and to keep his memory alive through a sport he truly loved and had played for so many years.

For Mike's third birthday game, I discovered a new ball field that would enhance the game-picnic celebration. The field could be seen from under the shelter and the park provided a much better bleacher seating section. "The Game" was evolving each year. And yet this was probably the most difficult to plan.

Mike's girlfriend, Megan, was killed on December 18, 2004, the day after her twenty-fifth birthday. She was buried two gravesites from Mike. The void and grief I felt made it unimaginable for me to continue with plans for the game; I was completely immobilized. Earlier, I had agreed to do sweat equity to minimize the cost of obtaining the shelter and the field. Mike's friends – Adam, Sean and Nelson – as well as my friend, Dagmar, offered to help. But still I found it devastating without Megan. Together we had shared our memories of Mike as we selected pictures for the cake and the "Mike's Essence" give-away pictures. Megan always ordered the cake and helped me with the address labels and invitation mailing. She was so much a part of the process. Somehow it was not the same without Megan.

One evening I was so distraught that I called Pete and expressed my reluctance to continue "The Game." Pete was adamant; we had to carry on, it was something we needed to do. He reminded me how many people counted on the game and shared something Nick's father had said; "The Game" was very important to Mike's group, because it was a positive way of dealing with their loss. It helped Pete to cope with his grief also. But still I felt too sad and distraught. While I was talking with Pete, two of Mike's buddies called to say they would be at the park on Saturday to help with the sweat equity. Then a third call came in from Amanda asking me when "The Game" was this year. All of this took place while I put Pete on hold, something I never did. In amazement I returned to Pete and stated emphatically, "The Game is on!" Obviously, Mike wanted "The Game" to continue, and with a little help from our friends, I knew this would definitely continue to be an annual event. The conviction was reinforced as others stepped forward with offers to help. I realized how remarkable and supportive all of our friends were – Pete's, Mike's and my own dear friends and family who understood the significance of the celebration. I was truly blessed.

The third year was even better than before. I relieved Ron from sweating over hot charcoals by ordering fried chicken, potato salad and cole slaw for the picnic. I took on the responsibility of the birthday cake. Another friend of Mike's, known as "the other Megan" came out to the house with her husband CJ to pick up bottled water and supplied ice chests for the game. Helen and Dagmar (I can't image what I'd do without them) continued to help monitor the picnic and set out food. This year Ms. Darcy's (as she was known to Pete and Mike) infamous sugar cookies became a favorite and another tradition began. When Pete and Mike were young, she cared for the boys after school until I returned home from work. Darcy often let the boys make sugar cookies and pick out their own favorite color sugar for the topping. The cookies brought a fond memory that only Pete really understood and valued. Aunt T was there with her cash box collecting the money and updating addresses and phone numbers. How could I have doubted this is what I was supposed to do when I had so much support, love and encouragement from those who cared?

Everything just fell into place by the fourth year and I knew it would be easier each year. Everyone seemed to know the routine now and they took their places on the field warming up, while catching up with old friends. Parents, families and friends continued to show up throughout the afternoon. More and more of the parents and girls now played in "The Game" and it had become quite a rivalry between *The Bigworms* and *The Weethees*. The list of Mike's friends who had passed on to the Other

Side had grown and this game was dedicated to "Our Angels in the Outfield" – Mike, Megan, Travis, Nick H., Adam J. and Samantha.

The official plaque is updated with the name of the winning team each year. I do believe this event will continue until the plaque is complete, and maybe longer. I've now excused myself from the real game since I realized the opposing team only let me get onto first base because I'm Ms. Ludman, Mike's mom, and I admit, I do run like a girl. Well, it was a special treat while it lasted. But now things are quite competitive and Mike would have liked that since he was very competitive himself. I still take an honorary bat when there is no chance I could be a detriment to the team. But that's fine with me. The previous year I almost made it home but was put out between third and home base. I told them that I'm supposed to get home. Well, that started a "fight" in the field and, although I knew it was the way the guys "messed" with each other, I swore I'd never do it again. I know I'll never get home, but they always let me get to first – that's a given. As Adam explained to Pete the next year, "Hey, man, we let your mom get to first and second, but we can't let her score!" And I totally understand. So I just have fun having my honorary bat and then go back to taking pictures and enjoying the game.

This past year was the seventh game. Aunt T, Helen and several others were not able to attend, but there are still so many who come out and help each year – Dagmar, my friend Amanda, Darcy and all the parents who bring goodies and have my back. This year there were many small children – children of players, grandchildren, nieces and nephews. One day these will be the players hearing stories about Mike and calling his friends the old guys and gals!

Just five weeks before the game we experienced another death – Mike's friend Ryan. As raw as they were, Ryan's wife and mother attended the game and the annual trophy was awarded to Ryan's wife in his memory. Two of Mike's friends made me realize how important it was to honor him. It was a very emotional moment, but deeply meaningful to all who were there to witness the underlying message of the game, and something Mike always did – take care of friends.

One of the girls was impressed with how many people attended the year before to show their love, respect and friendship for Mike, but was totally astounded this year to see all the old friends attending for the first time. They had lived out of town or for some reason had just heard about the game and wanted to be a part of it now, and in the years to come. She stated, "The game is a testament of how wonderful, special, loved and revered Mike truly was to everyone". Those words really describe how I feel every year.

Because of *The Mike Ludman Memorial Game,* Mike will be remembered and his life will live on with joy and enthusiasm while benefiting worthy causes at the same time. Each year I feel him smiling down and often laughing at some of the antics – for instance, the year Lou slid into home base and I knew because I could hear his head hit the plate, or the year Nelson brought the bottle of Remi Martin to toast Mike during the cake cutting, and of course, the year Adam cut the cake instead of Pete. Nelson kept looking at me across the picnic table asking if he could dunk Adam's head in the cake. Well, at first

I said "No," but when he asked the second time, I felt this idea was not coming from Nelson, but from Mike. I nodded an "okay" and then before I knew what was happening, there were three different hands smashing Adam's head into the cake. Obviously, no one had cake that year, but we had a great cake fight with even some of the parents participating. I just knew Mike loved the way this all played out and he was laughing and enjoying the camaraderie. There is something special about each year and I know Mike is always a part of the heart and soul of this extended family.

Mike's First Anniversary

As August of 2003 approached, I was facing my first birthday without Mike and the first anniversary of his death. I'll never forget the beautiful, meaningful, birthday card my mother sent me. When I opened the envelope I wept. A very cute brown haired, somber looking little boy of about four or five-years-old, dressed in a suit with a little brown cap appeared holding a bouquet of red roses. The words my mother wrote inside touched my heart. She said, "I guess he (Mike) found a way, a round about way, to send his Mom a birthday bouquet and let you know how much he cares." My family now understood there are no coincidences and believed Mike led my mother to this particular card.

A few days later I received an exquisite memory box made of dark, cherry wood with the inside lined in green felt. The box had Mike's name engraved on a bronze plaque atop the box. Here I would keep the things of his that I cherish. My whole family contributed and it meant so much to know they understood my pain and grief, even though they could never really "know." I appreciated their love and support. My birthday brought back so many memories of our family reunion the year before at T's house in Pensacola, when we shared so much fun, laughter and togetherness that will never be the same again.

The sadness engulfed me as I knew what was coming next – the first anniversary of Mike's death and there was nothing I could do to stop it. My anxiety level increased and I pleaded with God to help me live through this anniversary, one full of pain, grief and regret. Will I survive the memories and the heartache? I had decided months before to go to Wilmington and Carolina Beach to spread some of Mike's ashes in places he loved and where he had found peace, enjoyment and contentment. Megan wanted to be with me, and my sister Theresa flew in from New Orleans to be a part of the journey. We were determined to complete Mike's unfinished trip to Wilmington. Pete came in from Knoxville, but decided to stay in Charlotte to be with his dad and some of Mike's friends. This anniversary was also the birthday of Mike's good friend Adam.

Megan and I picked up T from the airport and headed to Wilmington. As we drove along Highway 74 and neared our destination, I noticed the time. It was 7:20 p.m. on Friday night, the time of Mike's accident the year before. The tears stung as they streamed down my cheeks and as I glanced into the rear view mirror I realized Megan had also noticed the time. She too was starting to cry. We finally pulled off the highway to let my sister drive the rest of the way – I could no longer concentrate on driving. I was reliving the night of August 16th, the night my life changed forever, the night my nightmare began with a phone call from a man who didn't even know my son or me. Megan and I were both thinking of what might have been and what we didn't want to face, the reason we were on this sorrowful and difficult journey for Mike, but without him, only Mike's ashes and his memory.

We settled into our hotel knowing the next steps would be a very hard – spreading Mike's ashes. I held onto that urn so tightly. I carried it everywhere we went – I even talked to the urn as if Mike was really with us.

After dinner at the same little seafood restaurant I'd visited before, we were on our way to Wrightsville Beach. We would spread some of Mike's ashes at the place where he hung out with his buddies, the same place Amanda and I experienced the awe-inspiring, meaningful sunset months before, while relaxing and enjoying the peace and serenity of the ocean spilling into the harbor.

We arrived equipped with our wine, coolers, beach towels and beach chairs to experience that "special" place on the beach. At first, we talked, laughed and told stories about Mike, trying to ignore the reason we were there. Megan went off to retrieve another bottle of wine from the car for T and me – she, herself, wasn't much of a drinker. While we sat chatting and reminiscing we noticed a set of headlights on the beach heading right for us. I panicked!

"Oh my God, someone is trying to kill us!" I exclaimed, as I jumped up. T ran for the ocean and I hid behind a flimsy beach chair. What was I thinking? T told me to run to the water and I started running back and forth, not knowing what escape would be our safe haven. I'm sure it appeared to be a scene from a 1930's black and white silent comedy film. As T and I comically ran back and forth between the ocean waves and the beach chairs, Megan returned. She knew what was happening. She dropped the bottle of wine in the sand dunes and walked up nonchalantly. The headlights stopped right before us and a young patrolman stepped out of his truck. Okay, now how do I explain this to the beach patrol? Well, I ran up to him and I announced that I thought he was trying to kill us! I was really off to a good start with the law. Then we introduced ourselves, explained the reason for our gathering at the beach and even asked if he would like to join us. It was unbelievable – he was such a nice guy and very understanding – his name was Shannon. He explained that we couldn't have alcohol on the beach, so I assured him we would get rid of the wine. He just smiled and said if we put the wine in the cooler he wouldn't *see* it and we could carry on with the our ceremony. I was so amazed and relieved that this young man could empathize with our journey and encourage us to "carry on." And then he left us to do what we came to do.

Our mood then changed dramatically, as we now had to face the reason we were at this specific place on the beach at this specific time. We became very quiet, aware of Mike's presence and just sat with our memories for a while. Then Megan broke the silence to confess that the guy she had been seeing when she and Mike had their last relationship problem was named Shannon! I was speechless and sad, but then I broke into uncontrollable laugher. Megan and T looked at me with astonishment and disbelief.

"Mikie didn't miss a trick," I exclaimed, while trying to explain my behavior. "He had his mom and Aunt T running around like fools to insure that we met a guy named Shannon!" Mike is good; he is very, very good. He wanted us to know he was there with us and enjoying the shenanigans with an "I got ya"!

The laughter died away, and once again we became silent. Slowly and solemnly, we walked to the ocean surf with Mike's ashes. We each took a handful and separated to spread his ashes, each in our own private way and each with our own private thoughts. The heaviness returned as we did what we came to do in honor of Mike – to leave a part of him here, in a place where he felt so much peace and love and laughter. Again, I was only with Mike's memories, not experiencing the moment with him in the physical – only in spirit.

When we returned to the hotel room I called Pete to tell him of our experience on the beach. I don't know what I was thinking; Pete was suffering with his own sadness and couldn't really understand why we felt this occurrence was so significant or why we were laughing and excited. How could he understand his mom's behavior?

On Saturday, Megan, T and I went to the Carolina Beach Fishing Pier to spread the rest of Mike's ashes. From a spot by the railing we each cast Mike's ashes and as they drifted through the coastal air, we watched them float on the sea breeze to the vast ocean waves below. We hugged each other and we cried. As we walked away I felt a silence and a reverence on the pier from all the fishermen as they sat fishing, but watching us with heads bowed to show their respect. We were so much in our own world that we didn't even think about how this might affect others on the pier. But I was surprised and felt at peace with the spirit of others' acknowledgement of what had just occurred.

In Wilmington, Megan showed us the first house Mike and his friends had rented. It was a nice three-bedroom house close to the University where Mike had made a lot of friends. Megan recounted stories of her trips to visit Mike and the parties they had attended. Mike wasn't much on bars but he enjoyed parties with friends. And often, I was told, he would forgo those parties for some time alone to just relax and talk at home with friends.

I was still learning so much about my son and his world as he left home to live independently. Of course, there were many more stories from his time in Wilmington I learned over the years, some at which I had to laugh, but at the same time felt as if I should have been there for him. Every young person has to go out into the world and experience it for themselves. It was that time in Mike's life for him and I didn't feel I should intrude. When I did call he might be on his way out the door to go bowling or at home playing poker with the guys. He was doing his thing.

That evening, we all dressed for dinner and Megan took us to a wonderful Italian restaurant, which had been very special to her and Mike. I could tell at times during dinner that it was extremely hard for Megan – memories of their time together were filling her heart. We carried on and enjoyed our dinner, but the night was much more sedate and quiet; there were too many thoughts and memories going through our minds.

On Sunday morning, the 17th, we realized we had done what we came to do and wanted to get back to Charlotte and to Pete. Pete had told us Nick's parents were having a cookout for Adam's birthday and that's where I wanted to be – with Pete and the boys, Mike's family. When we arrived Adam was blowing out the candles on his cake and most of the guys were there. It was difficult. We were celebrating Adam's birthday on Mike's anniversary. We talked and hugged and Nick's dad played a video of a baseball game from league ball when the guys were in junior high school. It brought a tear to my eye, as did seeing Nick on the sofa, paralyzed from the mid-chest down, with Serena by his side.

Pete, Megan and T had not yet forgiven Serena, but I knew it was an accident and Mike wanted me to forgive. Mike told me early on with Mary Beth that I was supposed to forgive the driver. A few days after the accident, Serena called me in tears, but I was at the funeral home making Mike's wake and funeral arrangements. She spoke with T, whom I'm sure was not very receptive; there was simply too much anger at that time. At the wake Serena approached me sobbing, saying how very sorry she was. At that moment I understood how guilty she felt for Mike's death, and how painful it was for her. I had forgiven her, although I didn't really feel it was necessary. Serena was only eighteen-years-old and she would have to live with the memory the rest of her life. I thought, "What if Mike had been driving and someone else was killed?" Could Mike live with that? It would change him forever. I did feel Nick felt a lot of guilt, but over the years I believe he knows he was not responsible.

That night Pete and Megan stayed up talking long after T and I went to bed. Megan spent the night and was the first person I allowed to sleep in Mike's bed. It felt right. Before that I had been the only one since the accident who fell asleep in his bed. After Megan's death, I learned from her mom, Patty, that Megan had called her during the night crying. She wanted to be there with us but it was very hard on her at the same time.

I made it through Mike's first anniversary with Pete, T, Megan, family and friends. But the next day, Pete had to leave for Knoxville, T left for New Orleans and Megan left for home. I was all alone again in my grief. I didn't have to put up a front. The tears, the memories and the silence returned. Now my life returned to the "new normal," although I had yet to figure out what that was. I went back to work, KinderMourn, my psychologist, my psychiatrist and my meds. I went back into my cave and my retreat from life until I could figure out how I could go on. I'd now been through all the "firsts" but soon realized time would not be the release for my heartache and sadness that I hoped it would be. Joy and enthusiasm were still so remote. The healing, I feared, would take a very long time – if ever.

Larkspur

Five months after Mike's accident, I awoke from a dream and wrote the words "Larkspur – houses on the marina." At the time those words had absolutely no meaning to me. My first thought the next morning was, "What the heck is Larkspur?" I searched the web and discovered it was a small town across the bay from San Francisco. The website opened with a photo of a statue of Don Quixote, which brought to mind the framed lithograph of Don Quixote I had given Mike for his first apartment. Sadly, it was one of his possessions that was still missing. There was a dazzling photo of the Larkspur marina at sunset, with a caption stating the marina is known for its houses which extend out over the water. I'd never heard of Larkspur before, yet I had spelled it correctly and even capitalized it when I scribbled it down during the night. I knew immediately this was no ordinary dream; it was a message, a message from Mike. I had no doubt I was going to Larkspur. I didn't know why or how, but I knew I was going.

I called a dear friend of mine, Patrice, whom I'd known since childhood, to share my dream experience and tell her that sometime soon I was going to a place called Larkspur. A few weeks later she phoned to ask when I was planning my trip. I've always liked the month of October and decided that was when I'd like to go. Patrice sounded excited and said a friend of ours from elementary and high school, Luncky (a nickname that still stuck), lived in Sacramento and had a cabin at Lake Tahoe. She wanted to invite five or six of the old gang for a trip to Lake Tahoe. Patrice said October would be perfect. She also mentioned Luncky had previously lived in Sausalito and passed the Larkspur marina often. This was the first inkling of signs that were to come – Luncky was married to a brain surgeon named Michael Edwards! Okay, this was getting interesting. On the next phone call Patrice had more definite plans. We would meet in San Francisco, stay in Larkspur for three nights and then head to Lake Tahoe for the next five nights. We'd finish the trip back in Larkspur. That worked for me. My only concern was getting there. I felt like Natalie Wood in *Miracle on 34th Street* as she rode away so disappointedly from the Christmas party – "I believe, I believe, I don't know why, but I believe!"

I was going to Larkspur. Why? I hadn't a clue, but I believed. In April, I found a great rate on an airline ticket to San Francisco and booked the flight to ensure that I was going, no matter what may happen with everyone else. There would be no change in my plans.

As October neared and everything fell into place, I remembered the open gallery with Mary Beth I had attended in January. At the time, the words she said to me made no sense. She asked if I was going on a trip. I said no. I had no plans for a trip, and vacation plans were the last thing on my mind. Mary Beth told me I would definitely be going on a trip, and from the symbol Mike was showing her, it was a gift from him. I thought he'd have to be pretty darn good to pull that off, but I have since learned I always have to be aware and to trust my gut instinct. Sometimes it takes a while to see the way things play out. When communicating with the Other Side there is no reason or logic, it is beyond our comprehension.

There were to be six of us – Luncky, Moosie, Patrice, Kiki, Eileen and me. I promise those are real people with nicknames that stuck and no one seems to remember their origin. I hadn't seen Luncky (Linda) since our twenty-year elementary school reunion in 1985. Moosie (Liz) and I had gotten together the previous Christmas when I was in New Orleans, but before that it had been years since we had seen each other. I saw Kiki (Colleen) then too, for the first time since 1996, which was the last time I had seen Eileen. Never in my wildest dreams could I have conjured up such a trip. All I did was make my plane reservations. Luncky and Patrice worked out all the details.

When I arrived in San Francisco, Luncky, Moosie and Patrice met my plane and we shouted enthused hellos and hugged in our excitement to be together again. Then off we went to Larkspur. Luncky graciously took care of our hotel accommodations at a hotel on the marina. She knew all the places to go, the great places to eat, and most importantly, how to get there. Luncky was our very own tour guide.

We awoke our first morning to a dreary, cool, foggy day, not unusual for the Bay Area. After breakfast at a cozy little coffee shop near the hotel, we hopped the ferry to cross the bay to San Francisco. There was excitement in the air and we were like children again, caught in a magical moment. We had a great play day – riding aboard the ferry with the wind blowing our hair straight atop our heads, riding the Merry-go-round at the pier's shopping village, riding the trolley from the pier to Fisherman's Wharf and then lunch and shopping. Luncky suggested Tarantino's for lunch, one of her favorite restaurants that overlooked the bay marina. As we took our seats I looked out at the small, peaceful marina and there it was – a small fishing boat named *Mike!* Not *Mike's Nautical Beauty* or any such seaworthy boat name, just *Mike!* He was definitely letting me know he was with me.

As we were shopping along the Wharf after lunch, Patrice stopped to check out some jewelry with one of the street vendors. She asked his name, since she wanted to think it over before she made her purchase. Both the vendor and another shopper answered, *"Mike!"* Then, as I sat on a bench listening to a musician serenade the tourists waiting to board the next trolley car, he ended his song and introduced himself as Peter something or other. Peter – Mike's big brother. Okay, could just be a coincidence. Yeah, right!

As we enjoyed chocolate sundaes at Ghirardelli Square, Patrice finally confessed this adventure was actually planned a few months after Mike's accident. She told Luncky she was sure I would never agree to a vacation to San Francisco and Lake Tahoe. She was right. I didn't do anything or go anywhere unless it involved Pete or Mike. Nothing else had any meaning or purpose. There was no joy anymore. Sadness overwhelmed me every hour of every day. My enthusiasm had evaporated. I still lived in a robot-like state just trying desperately to survive. I had no clue the trip was already in the works when I told Patrice about my dream, but she knew right then I was going and so did Mike.

Oh, he's good; he's very, very good, my Mikie. He knew I wouldn't go on a fun excursion, so he gave me a place called Larkspur and sent me on a mission. I guess that's the only way he felt he could get through to me. "Okay, Lovebug, you learned how to play the game and you're now making the rules for your Momma." When Mike was in school, if he had a problem with a teacher, I always told him to pay attention, find out their game, find out their rules and learn how to play their game. His brother Pete always knew how to play the game, but not Mike. It would have made life so much easier for him. But he had that impenetrable pride mixed with uncertainty! Respect – that was so important to Mike. He needed respect from others *before* he could go along with their game plans.

How clever. Mike sent his mom on a wonderful excursion, disguised as a mission. Oh, how very clever. It was all making sense now. I couldn't understand why I didn't feel an immediate connection to Larkspur as soon as I laid eyes on it. A little dramatic, I know, but that's how I had it played out in my head. The purpose? Well, yes, there was a purpose, but to my surprise it wasn't a spiritual quest, instead I was simply to go out into the world again, have fun and live my life. Never in all my dreams did I ever believe I could afford a trip like this. But it was really out of my control; Mikie had taken care of the details. He just had others involved and working on the plans for his Momma. Most of the expenses were covered, which I wasn't even aware of until I was leaving for San Francisco. I only knew I was supposed to go. Mike had always been generous and he's no different now on the Other Side. But Mike also liked acknowledgement. He wanted to know that his efforts were appreciated. He definitely left no doubt he had orchestrated this trip for me; it truly was a gift from Mike.

The next day was a sunny California day. We had breakfast at one of those charming, healthy, Sausalito restaurants and headed for Muir Woods. The dank, green forest was quite an adventure. The huge, massive redwoods appeared to reach the sky, and the strong bouquet from the woodland made us feel as if we were in a sanctuary, engulfed in anther world, a million miles from anywhere. It was totally awesome! We walked the trail, a little longer than I originally anticipated, and ran into some young twenty-somethings hiking in search of the bar at the top of the trail. Somebody got them good! Of course, one of the fellows was named *Mike* and another was wearing one of Mike's trademarks, a Nautica tee shirt. But still, not really unusual, mostly an uneventful day as far as Mikie-sightings were concerned.

On Saturday we headed for Lake Tahoe to meet Kiki and Eileen at Luncky's cabin. Her *cabin* was a lovely three-bedroom home nestled among the towering, green pine and fir trees located along a serene, winding mountain road. Oh, yes. It was a little piece of heaven. We decided on an early dinner in town at a restaurant overlooking the glimmering, dark blue lake. The weather was gorgeous, with clear blue skies, bright warm sunshine and just a hint of the cool crisp chill of October. As we waited for the restaurant to open, Patrice, Kiki and I went out to enjoy the view from the balcony. Wow, what a great photo op! I started to take a picture of them when a young man, who was enjoying the afternoon eating ice cream with his girlfriend, approached me. He suggested he take the picture of all three of us. Great! He asked where we lived. When I told him I was visiting from North Carolina, he said they had just returned from a vacation there.

"What part?" I asked.

"Wilmington," he answered, as Patrice and I gasped and looked at each other.

"What's your name?" Patrice questioned anxiously.

"Michael!"

We knew the answer before we heard it. We just shook our heads, smiled and laughed. Patrice was starting to understand just what I meant when I talked about messages from Mike and how he was always with me. She was now witnessing it first-hand. I literally felt warm all over and so content. The six of us had a great evening lounging around, drinking wine, catching up and reminiscing about old times. We laughed so hard. It was as if all the years in-between had never eluded us and I definitely needed laughter in my life again.

Sunday began with a magnificent, crisp, fall morning. We were lazily drinking coffee and having a casual breakfast when Patrice floated into the comfy, inviting living room and exclaimed what a great morning it was.

"What's that song? *Morning has broken . . . dah dah dah dah . . .*"

We all joined in as we picked up the chorus of the 1970s Cat Stevens song, *Morning Has Broken.* There was an ease in being together which felt so perfect and I thought, "It doesn't get much better than this." Since it was Sunday, we wanted to go to the eleven o'clock mass. We all grew up together in New Orleans and went to Catholic schools. Although I was no longer a practicing Catholic, it was a given we would attend mass.

The picturesque church had a full-length glass wall behind the altar, which overlooked the tranquil, wooded landscape. You could feel the peace and you could hear the quiet. Then it was announced the opening hymn would be *Morning Has Broken* and Father Mike would say the mass! Again, Patrice and I smiled and shook our heads knowingly. Mike was making sure no one missed his presence. He continued to reassure me I was supposed to be on this trip.

The next day we embarked on another daylong excursion to the old, historic mining town of Virginia City. On the way, we stopped at an overlook for another photo op to take a picture of the dry, desert like mountains spread upon a sea of rock and brush. Patrice and I were still lingering, as the others walked to the cars, when a young couple approached, so we asked them to take a picture of us surrounded by a huge cave-like rock on the outcrop. The young man took our picture and as we started to walk along the path, Patrice turned and asked his name.

"Nathan," he answered.

Patrice was so relieved. "Thank God!" she exclaimed, "Not another Mike."

"Well, not really," I answered, then explained how Mike's name actually was Nathan for the first six days of his life before his dad asked to have it changed to Michael. She looked at me with disbelief and later confessed she thought I had concocted the explanation. But it didn't matter. I knew and that was all that Mike needed – for me to know.

Mike's signs kept me enthused and motivated each day as I enjoyed my time with old friends, but I began to feel overwhelmed by all the activity. I had been jolted from my self-imposed seclusion and isolation and eventually I wanted and needed my alone time. I stayed behind as the others went out shopping. I found myself alone some evenings, just sitting and rocking on the front porch. Everyone seemed to understand, although it was unspoken, and they let me have some time to myself to cry. The downs sometimes seemed to take over the ups, but I was still so grateful for my fantastic trip.

It was finally time for some of the group to leave us. On Wednesday, Kiki and Eileen left for Reno to return home. The rest of us spent a delightful, sunny day on a guided tour cruising the deep-blue waters of Lake Tahoe. The clear, blue sky and the cool breeze added to the relaxing conclusion of our stay in Lake Tahoe – a day to contemplate the beauty of life, a day to take it all in and be thankful for the opportunity to get a glimpse of the kind of life I once enjoyed.

Then, alas, it was time to part. Moosie, Patrice and I made our way back to San Francisco for one more evening before our departure. After sightseeing, we parked at a meter which forced us to run back every so often to fill it with coins. As we continued on our shopping journey along Fisherman's Wharf, Patrice noticed a security guard in an alley between two restaurants. I still can't imagine what prompted her to stop and talk to him. She returned with a big, satisfied smile and was quite happy. Patrice explained that the security guard said his boss would be leaving in a few minutes so we could park there and he would watch the car for us. Now why would someone do that for a couple of tourists? She and I went in search of the car – we forgot to notice the name of the street where we had originally parked. After finally locating it we headed to the Wharf and parked right there in the midst of the tourist venue. The guard couldn't have been nicer, but I wanted to know his name just in case we were questioned about parking there and he was nowhere in sight when we returned.

"*Mike!*" he said, with a big grin.

Patrice gasped and said I *had* to tell him. By this time he probably thought we were escaped criminals or worse. So I gave him a brief explanation of our Mikie sightings. He just beamed and puffed out his chest and said, "That's why I'm here – to look after you." My Mikie had really outdone himself this time.

After meeting Moosie and more shopping, we decided to have dinner at Tarantino's, the same restaurant overlooking the Marina – the one with the *Mike* boat. We were in store for a very big finale from Mike. We were not quite sure what to make of our waiter and his very strange sense of humor. He was teasing us in a very mischievous manner, for example, he brought me a glass of coke in a wine glass, instead of the red wine I'd ordered, and then he took a sip and exclaimed how good it was. The three of us were dumbfounded. I kept asking, "Did he really take a sip of my wine?" As I lifted my glass to drink he hurried to the table with my real glass of wine and explained that the other glass was Coke. Then he walked away shaking his head and laughing. What was this all about?

Before we entered the restaurant we noticed a character out on Fisherman's Wharf earning his living by jumping out from behind a fake bush and scaring the daylights out of people. We questioned our waiter about this fellow's strange antics. His only explanation was that the wacky fellow had been in the same spot for twenty-three years. As we probed for more information, his only response was, *"Twenty-three years!"* As the waiter was serving another table, Patrice glanced over and caught his eye. From across the room he said again, *"Twenty-three years!"* We were more curious than ever and still enthralled with how outlandish and bizarre his behavior was. We wondered why he acted so strangely. When we asked for the check, once more Patrice tried to ply the waiter for information about the Wharf character, but again all we got was, *"Twenty-three years!"* When the peculiar waiter brought our check, *"23 years!"* was written across the front in black marking pen. "Whatever!" was all we could think and we left the restaurant perplexed.

Once on the road, Patrice pulled over to reread the directions to our hotel. As we pulled away from the curb I noticed we were across the street from Pier 23. It finally hit me.

"Oh my God!" I blurted out. *"Twenty-three!* That's Mikie's number!"

I explained that Mike had the number twenty-three early in his baseball career and he used it for all his codes, such as his phone and pager code with his buddies, his computer code, etc. It was also part of my computer password – *Mikie23*. I told them now that I'd figured it out we wouldn't see that number again the rest of the trip. Mike usually stops using a particular sign once I catch on.

"I knew we should have kept that check!" Patrice exclaimed.

Back in Charlotte, my friend Dagmar picked me up from the airport the next evening. We went to dinner at one of Mike's favorite restaurants, where Pete, Megan and I had celebrated his last birthday dinner with him. As I recounted all the messages from Mike that occurred during my trip, she was in awe, but not surprised. Dagmar had witnessed and heard of many of the signs Mike sent to me. And she believed.

As I entered my house the first thing I saw was a red rose in the nook between the living room and the kitchen. Then I saw a vase on the dining room table with about two-dozen multi-colored roses and a Josh Groban CD. One song was highlighted, *To Where You Are*. That would become a very significant song for me from that point on. As I walked through the house, I found a vase with another dozen roses on my bathroom counter. Dagmar and I looked at each other and at the same time exclaimed, "Helen!" Mike did some of his best work through my dear friend Helen. I was welcomed home with love.

I was surrounded with blessings and gifts, extraordinary trips, friendships and love. My friend, Joanna, had given me a lovely photo journal for my birthday. She said it was to begin my new life, starting with photos from my trip to Larkspur. To my circle of friends, this trip was no coincidence, it was no accident, it was no frivolous excursion. They understood, as I did, it was a gift from Mike to show me he wanted me to move forward and get on with my life. I didn't need anyone else to interpret my messages from Mike. He and I were beginning to communicate on a different level, one that we will use for the rest of my life. It was a gift that exceeds all comprehension, yet so very blatant, so very connected. It was a symbol of an ending and a symbol of a beginning.

My Escape to Seascape

It didn't take long for my bleak reality to surpass the highs I experienced in October. By early November 2003, I realized I was broken and needed time to be alone and grieve my son's death. I felt I was losing my mind as well as my desire to live. Everything was different now. I found myself wanting desperately to be with Mike, yet I still wanted to be with Pete. I felt insane, lost and in despair. I didn't know which way to turn. I didn't know what to do to keep my sanity.

My psychologist, Brian, decided to write me out of work, under my short term disability policy, for a few months to find my way without the pressures and obligations that came with my job. The work environment kept me feeling isolated and disconnected. What Brian didn't realize was I needed to run away during that time and he was not happy with my decision. He didn't feel I needed to be so isolated and made appointments for me to return to Charlotte for semi-monthly sessions. I just wanted and needed time to be away from all the memories and all the constant reminders. How ironic, yet inevitable, that I decided to go to the Wilmington area where Mike had lived before returning home for our last few months together. My KinderMourn counselor, Elizabeth, along with the rest of the group, supported my decision, but wanted me to keep in touch and Elizabeth even set up a conference call so I could participate in the session on New Year's night. I was also encouraged to take along the dramatic oil painting I recently discovered at a florist shop.

While purchasing a red rose on my way to the cemetery during one of my long lunch hours, I noticed an oil painting high on the wall above the flower arrangements. As soon as I saw it, I "knew" it was meant for me. It was the inspiration for my trip. The painting portrays three calla lilies, all in different stages of development. I felt the fully opened blossom represented Mike, the half opened one was Pete and I was the lily, with the teardrop on the long stem, still struggling to open. The flowers stood out against a dark-stained wooden wall with a window opened to a raging sea under a moonlit night sky. I was stunned. The painting depicted sadness, loneliness and a sense of turmoil. It was a reflection of where I was at the time and I knew it was my message to go to the sea. I needed the healing power of the ocean.

I left on my journey in the beginning of December to an oceanfront condo on Carolina Beach, within walking distance of the Carolina Fishing Pier. It was very near Wilmington and also a little less expensive. I packed my bags and escaped, in hopes of finding some release. My "angel friend," Helen, saw me off, with a large, bountiful basket filled with all the essentials she felt I needed for my trip – Kleenex, toilet paper, chocolates, spices, note pads, pens, etc. It was so like Helen, "Go, but take care of yourself." She, too, was worried about my decision, yet she honored what I felt was necessary. I left Charlotte, and as always, whenever I traveled back and forth to Carolina Beach, I started a Marvin Gaye CD and said, "Okay, Mike, let's go!"

I'd been at the beach for a week before it finally hit me – my condo was Seascape 17. Mikie left us on the seventeenth and that number was very significant to me now. I don't know why it took me so long to realize, the number was staring me in the face each time I walked up the three flights of stairs to the door. A few days after my arrival, I noticed some items needing repair and called the realty agent. Her husband came by to make the repairs and we started talking. He and his wife had lost their son two years prior and had left their home to move to Carolina Beach. He also told me a woman about my age had rented a condo a few blocks away; she had lost her son in Iraq the past summer. Another coincidence? Oh, now this was getting interesting – why did I choose this particular place where I would be in contact with other bereaved parents? The very thing I was trying to escape. I gave him my number and told him if she felt like talking she could contact me.

At first I felt really lonely and strange, but I woke each day to the sight of my painting on the bedroom wall and would read my Mikie journal out on the balcony, bundled in a jacket, hat and gloves to withstand the cold ocean breezes. Then I would sit at the small kitchen table and write. A few days later I had an especially good day – it was cold and windy, but also bright and sunny. I found a Unity church and decided to attend that morning.

It would be only the fourth time I'd attended a church since Mike left. The first was with the priest who gave Mike the Last Rites and officiated at his Celebration of Life. He performed a private mass a few days after the funeral, for Pete, Mike's dad and me. We sat around a small table on the altar. It was a very intimate, personal and powerful service. The next occasion was our first Christmas season without Mike, when Pete and I were in New Orleans. The mass intention was for Mike at St. Pius (the same church where both the boys were baptized), so Pete and I attended with his grandmother and other family members. During the entire mass, I gripped Pete's hand as the tears rolled down my cheeks. I wanted to be there, but I didn't want to be there. Then, the mass at Lake Tahoe in October, at the quaint, picturesque church situated amongst the soaring evergreen trees, where the mass was said by Father Mike. Now I decided to try the Unity church while on my *sabbatical* from work. I used to be such a connected part of a church family and I enjoyed the community, involvement and the stimulating sermons. But that part of my life now seemed irrelevant.

As I took my seat the church ensemble played *I'll be Home for Christmas*. Tears started flowing and I felt it was probably a good idea to get up and leave. But I stayed. After a short meditation, the minister proceeded to give his sermon. The theme was that in life there really are no accidents, all things lead us to our greater good, no matter how hard it is to understand at the time. His analogy referenced a recent trip to New Orleans (of all places – my hometown) at Thanksgiving. He and his friends were looking forward to a tour of New Orleans' Uptown Garden District Homes, but for some reason the tour was cancelled. They set out on a self-guided tour and accidentally found themselves in front of a house which looked exactly like a house from an Anne Rice novel. A limousine suddenly appeared with none other than Anne Rice herself, his friend's favorite author. She kindly consented to a photo and they went on their way, but not before realizing they had never conceived of the possibility of meeting Anne Rice. Their good fortune was the result of what they believed to be a big disappointment.

Still another coincidence. I had recently watched a television show about Anne Rice and how drastically her life had changed after the death of her six-year-old daughter. I had also viewed the John Edward's *Crossing Over* segment with Anne Rice, where he connected with her daughter. I felt I was supposed to meet her, not as a fan, but as one bereaved mother to another. Patrice's husband held a very important position in Anne Rice's literary empire. I had never before considered asking to meet Anne Rice, and I knew I never would, but the notion was enticing. I was very confident being in the Unity church that day was no mistake.

After the service I spoke with the minister to let him know how meaningful his sermon was for me. He directed my attention to the lady behind me and told me she had also lost her son the previous year. She and I spoke for several minutes, while barely holding back our tears, and then exchanged phone numbers. She had another son who had graduated from the University of North Carolina in

Charlotte and lived very close to my home. Coincidences? As the minister said, and I've heard so many times before, *"There are no accidents."* I knew this to be true, because they had been happening to me for many months.

As I left the church the street looked very familiar and I stumbled upon the little restaurant Mike's friend Amanda had introduced me to the year before – The Salt Works. This was an old Wilmington landmark, frequented by college students, families and just about anyone. It was an informal "turkey and dressing with two sides for $6.50" kind of restaurant, with a continuous turn over, serving breakfast, lunch and dinner. Amanda told me Mike really liked the place and used to eat there often. So I bought myself a Sunday newspaper and joined the crowd. While waiting for lunch my cell phone rang. I usually don't answer my phone in a public place, but then I saw the caller's number – it was Patrice. She and Moosie just called to say "hello" and see how I was doing. I knew this, too, was no accident. I had just been thinking about her during the Anne Rice story.

It was strange. I usually feel so self-conscious eating in a restaurant alone, but that day I felt totally relaxed, as if I belonged there. As I pulled out of the tree-shaded parking lot, I remembered this road also led to Wrightsville Beach. So on I went. It was a delightful, sunny day, if you discounted the cold and the wind. I felt good and I headed for the beach. I went directly to the sound where the boats enter the harbor – the place where Amanda and I witnessed the awe-inspiring sunset and dolphins playing in the surf, the place Megan, T and I spread Mike's ashes on the anniversary of his transition, the place Mike had his Aunt T and me running around like fools, because we thought someone was trying to run us over and the place Mike and his friends used to hang out – a place I wished I had shared with Mike, instead of with only memories of him. It's funny how meaningful that stretch of beach has become to me.

The afternoon turned extremely bitter and blustery. I had been complaining about the wind since I arrived at Carolina Beach but again, it finally struck me. Mikie said he would come to me in the wind. He'd definitely been around since I arrived. As I walked the beach I found the biggest, unmarred seashells I'd ever seen. They were gifts, keepsakes from Mike to take back with me. They sit in a large, green decorative piece on my living room coffee table as a constant reminder of my "run away" where numerous mystical and unworldly happenings occurred.

Later that afternoon, I bundled up again and walked down past the pier where only the untouched sand dunes separated the ocean from the harbor. I had my heart set on a dazzling sunset on the bay. While sitting on the dunes watching the sun descend behind the enormous harbor houses, I turned to take a look at the deep, blue sea. Again, I received a lesson that things don't always turn out as we plan. Instead of a splendid sunset, I was given a glorious view of the vast sea, painted with a pinkish hue just above the horizon and just below a clear, bright full moon. I had a hard time pulling myself away from the warmth of that scene to the comfort of my temporary haven. Once inside, I stepped out on the balcony to behold the moon shining brightly on the ocean. The rays of the moon made part of the ocean appear as a lake of light that led directly to my balcony with twinkling, white lights shimmering upon the swells before forming waves and crashing to the shore.

I would have remained glued to that balcony all night if it had been sixty-eight instead of thirty-eight degrees. My face and hands were numb before I admitted I needed to defrost and tomorrow was another day – another day with more awakenings to be realized. I told Mike, "Thanks for today. These are the days that help me go on."

By the middle of the second week I was feeling lonely and thought I should go back home. I decided I would only stay if Tess, the lady who lost her son in Iraq, called before Friday. Thursday night the house phone rang – it was Tess. We talked for a very long time and agreed to meet for dinner the next evening. She had also come to Carolina Beach to heal and deal with her "new normal." I knew it wasn't my time to leave. I remained through the middle of March and everything that happened there was so significant and healing for me. Tess was truly a blessing – I was not alone. We shared our feelings of despair, helplessness, hopelessness, pain and isolation that we experienced daily from this place in time without our sons. Who knew? I was in Carolina Beach to escape and came face to face with my struggle. Tess and I were both in Carolina Beach for the same reason – to escape the inescapable.

At first, Tess and I tiptoed around the signs from our sons, but those revelations brought us even closer. My sister, Mary Lee, had given me a book for Christmas the year before called, *Quit Kissing My Ashes* by Judy Collier. I identified with the author's loss of her son and the messages she received from him through psychic-medium Mary Jo McCabe. I was so impressed with what

Mary Jo McCabe had told her that I became determined to contact her myself. Since our session was by phone, there was no way she could have known the things she told me. I even received one message from Tess' deceased son that amazed both of us.

My first conversation with Mary Jo began with the appearance of a young man with strawberry blond hair and the initial "K" or "C." His name sounded like Christ or Chris and he showed her summer months of June or July. He then conveyed a message, which I didn't understand. It wasn't until later, as I was telling Tess, that it became clear. When she heard the message from this young man she began to cry. That connection was meant for her, and only she understood the meaning. Her son was killed in Iraq in July and his last name was Christian!

When Mary Jo finally found Mike, he was showing her a sword (I had just purchased a St. Michael visor medal for my car which depicted St. Michael with a sword) and then he referred to something that happened in mid-October, which brought him great pleasure and was a milestone for me. That could only be the trip he manipulated for me with my childhood friends to Larkspur. As I said before, Mike likes to be acknowledged and he was making sure I understood the trip was his gift to me. He wants me to move on and live again. Maybe I needed to get back to my roots in order to move forward. I hadn't really thought of that before, but it makes so much sense.

Mary Jo said Mike left this world suddenly and tragically, and he was now saying "Good-bye." He felt as if he never really got the chance to say good-bye. He also showed her his class ring. Recently I had learned that he lost the ring one night while partying with friends on Wrightsville Beach. To me, that meant Mike was acknowledging my visits to Wrightsville Beach and my knowing he had lost the ring there. Mary Jo then said, "Mike's rubbing his head." She asked if he was hard headed, which was somewhat true, but this was the way Mike first appeared to Pete shortly after his accident and it was the head injury which caused his death.

Mike showed Mary Jo a Christmas tree with him helping me string the lights. After Pete left for college, Mike always helped me decorate, and it brought tears to my eyes as I remembered our special times together decorating. She then said Mike was showing her a cookbook. Just the week before, my sister Theresa and I were discussing the upcoming holiday menu and I told her I wanted to make Mike's favorite, macaroni and cheese. I do believe Mike wants me to celebrate Christmas again.

There were many significant things Mary Jo told me which had to have come from Mike – she couldn't have known otherwise. She referred to the years 1988 and 1989, saying I gave up everything and had hard years after a big change. Those were the years when Ed and I separated and then divorced. They were very difficult for all of us, but Mike took it especially hard, withdrawing from sports and all the things he enjoyed in life. She continued that 1992 also brought a tremendous change for me. That was the year I joined the Unity church and attended various classes, which brought me healing and the beginning of a new life with new friends. Then Mary Jo stated that in 2002 everything changed dramatically in my life. All I could feel at the time was, "You think?" That was the year of Mike's accident, the year he left us and life, as we all knew it, changed forever.

Mary Jo gave me one more piece of information, which I found very reassuring and comforting. She said a family ancestor named Gladys was watching over Mike. I was clueless at the time, but later my mother told me about her Great Aunt Gladys, a kind and gentle person whom she liked very much. My mother sent me a picture of Gladys and she matched Mary Jo's description perfectly – she was a short, stout woman with grey hair pulled tightly in a bun. Her smile was genuine and sweet. After the session I remembered another psychic telling me Mike's angel was with him at the accident – the angel's name was Gladys.

Then came the words I always hated to hear, "Mike's gone."

How Strong Does God Think I Am?

My sabbatical was over and it was now time to return to work. I really didn't fit in anymore and wasn't made to feel welcome by some of my colleagues. I ran into an old colleague while exercising one day at the YMCA and we decided to meet for lunch. We hadn't seen each other or talked in years. After lunch Teresa and I visited my old department where I talked with several ex-colleagues and a previous team leader who mentioned an open position for a credit underwriter. Mary Jo McCabe had told me I would be led to a new position by a person named Teresa. At the time, I thought she meant Tess, whose real name is Teresa. By the end of March, I was hired back to my previous division, but it took several months before I realized it was *this Teresa* that Mary Jo had referred to, and not Tess. As I said before, sometimes it does take me a while to put the pieces together.

I resettled back into consumer credit with a wonderful, caring team leader. There were still many mornings when I sat in my car for several minutes waiting for the tears to abate before entering the building and putting on my "front." Whenever I drove, it seemed as if my mind would go back to the place where the movie reels played and the tears would follow. I was still in a state of confusion and grief, but I felt much more comfortable and included with this group of people. I was back in touch with old friends and co-workers, and although I knew the underwriting drill, there were still numerous changes to embrace. What else is new?

On a morning in July, I awoke with terrible stomach pains; my whole body ached. I decided to go to work, but as the day progressed, I regressed. By early afternoon, the fever and the stomach pains increased. My manager insisted I go to see my doctor. After a blood test and a brief examination, he ordered a CAT scan, since he felt the problem was caused by my appendix and I would probably have surgery that evening. Dagmar lived nearby and I called her to ask if she would take me to the hospital. As I waited for the chalk-like liquid to take effect for the scan, the pain became unbearable. My feisty friend insisted I be taken to the emergency room while waiting for the scan. The nurse injected two doses of morphine into my stomach, but to no avail. "What kind of diluted morphine are these people giving me?" I asked. The morphine did nothing for the pain. I noticed the look of concern on Dagmar's face and tried to alleviate her anxiety. I told her, "Don't worry, it couldn't be my appendix, because after all this time I would be dead already!"

After the scan the diagnosis came back – it was diverticulitis. "What now?" I thought bitterly. As the nurse wheeled the gurney down the hall, she informed me I would be in the hospital for several days and that I was fortunate since there was only one hospital room available, room 430. Dagmar and I just gasped and laughed. Mike's birthday – April 30th! The nurse looked at us as if we were crazy, but that's okay – I was just a "little unwell." I had no idea how dangerous this diagnosis was and thought I'd be leaving in the morning, but the night nurse made it clear this was no trivial matter.

In the morning a nurse entered the room to take some blood samples. When I arrived my blood count was twenty-two (whatever that meant - I only knew it wasn't good). I hated hospitals and I wanted out. I asked the "blood lady" what the blood count had to be in order to go home. She answered, "Ten to twelve, and that should take a few days." But who can get well in a hospital? I felt certain Mike had to be with me, because in less than forty-eight hours the blood count decreased to twelve, which surprised the nurses. When my neighbor arrived to bring me a few things I'd requested, I was sitting on the bed, dressed and ready to go home. Gwen looked startled until I explained I was released from the hospital. As we headed out the door, the doctor appeared with my discharge papers. She was quite taken aback to see I was leaving the hospital before I had officially been discharged. I signed the release papers, took my prescriptions and got the heck out of Dodge.

I tried, unsuccessfully, to return to work the next week. Being home sick just added to my depression and I was out of the office for three weeks. I would have to change my eating habits and watch my diet, but this disease still felt minor compared to all the anguish and life changes I'd already endured. I could live with this dis-ease, but I wasn't ready to live with what came next – breast cancer!

I went for my annual mammogram on my lunch hour in late September and was asked to wait for a sonogram after the x-rays. I was alarmed and anxious when the doctor was brought in to perform a biopsy. But I really became concerned when the nurse hugged me as I was leaving. When I got back to the office I told my colleague, Rose, I felt something was wrong because the nurse hugged me. She laughed because it sounded silly. But I knew. That nurse knew I was going to receive a phone call from my doctor very soon – another God-awful phone call.

The call came a few days later while I was at work. My gynecologist was very straightforward and professional – no nonsense, just the cold, hard facts, Jack. "You have breast cancer and I've set an appointment for you to see a surgeon next week." I burst into tears. How strong did God think I was? I felt angry and powerless. I was sent home and on the way I picked up two bottles of wine. When I got home, I wept as I envisioned a terrifying death ahead for me – a long, slow, painful death. I don't know where I found the courage, but I finally picked up the phone to call Pete. It was ironic. Since Mike's death I thought I wanted to die so I wouldn't feel the pain and heavy sadness. But now, faced with my own possible death, came the epiphany! I did want to release the grief, but I didn't want to die and leave Pete. I was now concerned about how Pete would accept the news. We talked for a long time, but it was hard to tell what was actually going through Pete's mind during our conversation. He tried to be strong and encouraging. I don't think Pete could really deal with the news. It felt to me as if he needed to detach in some way.

As I began processing the diagnosis, I had lots of questions and I called the doctor the next day. He was out of the office and another physician returned my call – a caring, kind, compassionate man. We talked for a long time as he discussed options and issues that lay ahead. He even spoke of his wife's challenges with breast cancer and seemed to understand my emotional state. Guess who's my doctor now?

Helen accompanied me to the surgeon's office for support and for another pair of ears to hear the surgeon's recommendations. The news sounded somewhat promising – the tumor was small and the cancer appeared to be contained. I would have a lumpectomy followed by radiation. I knew I'd never consent to chemotherapy and I felt a twinge of hope. I would be okay.

Lesley came to stay with me for the surgery and to care for me during the week. The surgery went well; the surgeon only took two lymph nodes since he felt the cancer was contained. I felt much more self-assured until I attended a clinic a week later to receive the test results on the lymph nodes. Cancer was found in one of the lymph nodes, which meant the cancer had possibly escaped into my blood stream. I was told I needed three chemotherapy treatments and then six weeks of radiation. More tears, anger and depression overpowered me. I couldn't understand why God was giving me so many trials.

Hope resurfaced on my follow-up appointment with the surgeon. We discussed options and he recommended an oncologist he knew, whom he believed would be open to what I felt I needed to do with the cancer treatments. The oncologist was a wonderful, compassionate doctor who talked with me for an hour and agreed to treat me with only the six-week radiation treatments.

During those six weeks I had two *dreams* – dreams that were not really dreams, but revelations and images that occur when a different level of consciousness is reached – one that opens access with the Other Side. One evening, during a deep meditation at the end of a yoga class, I found myself in that other dimension. Tears welled up in my eyes as I saw a full color scene of Mike and me sitting on a large rock in the mountains with a glorious waterfall nearby. Mike wore his blue Nautica shirt and blue jeans and he was very serious. He was trying to explain something to me, something important he wanted me to understand. When the yoga instructor guided the class out of meditation I didn't want to leave. There was something I was supposed to hear and as much as I tried, I couldn't hear what Mike was trying to tell me. I cried all the way home in silence, just trying to make sense of it. A week later, I woke up startled in the middle of the night with the insight, "It's not going to be a long drawn out affair – it will be quick, like a gunshot." It was a very disturbing thought, since I believed Mike was talking about me. I was to understand the message all too soon. It wasn't about me.

As the days grew into weeks, I began to feel the effects of the five-day per week radiation treatments. I tried to stay positive and during the treatments I would envision the radiation as little Pac-man angels gobbling up all the cancer cells. The fatigue was increasing and the burning of my skin was reaching a painful level – one I could live with, but painful nonetheless. Again, Helen came to take care of me and give moral support and by the last two weeks she was taking me for my treatments each day.

Christmas was fast approaching and I definitely was not in the mood to celebrate. Between the soreness and fatigue and no Mikie, I would be glad when the season was over. And still there in the back of my mind were the recent revelations that I believed were in reference to me. I wrestled with them constantly, but didn't tell anyone about my experience. Pete and I still didn't feel we could celebrate Christmas at home without Mike and I considered the notion that this could be the last Christmas for me. So despite the effects of the radiation, I still planned on being in New Orleans for Christmas, leaving on Christmas Eve, the day after I completed radiation. I needed to be with Pete and my family.

Sadly, the messages became crystal clear. On the Saturday before Christmas, Megan and I were to get together to exchange Christmas gifts and catch up with each other. At the last minute she called to postpone our get-together until later in the week, since she had been out the night before with friends to celebrate her twenty-fifth birthday. It was Saturday, December 18, 2004. Helen was hosting a Christmas dinner and gift exchange for the Woo Woos (my family of friends). I stopped to visit Mike around six-thirty on my way to Helen's. It was a fun evening with good friends, but I retired early due to the heaviness of fatigue. I had already arranged to spend the night, so it was easy to excuse myself from the rest of the evening's festivities. As I lay in bed, a huge sadness engulfed me, but I chalked it up to fatigue and seasonal sentiment. I arrived home early Sunday afternoon and turned on the television. The twenty-four hour news channel came on and the first thing I heard took my breath away. Surely, I couldn't have heard correctly! The news report was about the murder of Megan Miles the evening before around 6:30 p.m. I ran for the phone. In tears and angst I listened to another shocking, dreadful phone message.

"Ms. Ludman, this is Deanna, Megan's friend. Mrs. Miles asked me to call you. I regretfully inform you that Megan was killed last night." As Deanna broke into tears, I fell to my knees sobbing in a daze of disbelief and the eerie fog engulfed me once again. It was too incredible to comprehend. I called my sister, T. She and Megan had been close and talked occasionally by phone. Megan and Mike had also visited her several times in Pensacola. We both sobbed and tried to comfort each other. I then called Helen. She asked if I needed her to stay with me and I said no. I thought I'd get it together. I lit candles all through the house and opened my Mikie Journal and began to write, trying to make sense of it all. An hour later the doorbell rang. Of course, it was Helen. She knew this would be very difficult and confusing for me. She knew Megan's death would put me back in the heavy darkness. She stayed with me throughout the week and the next afternoon took me to place a red rose at the site where Megan was killed.

Megan was waked on Wednesday evening, the same day of the week and at the same funeral home where Mike was waked. Earlier, I asked Megan's mom, Patty, if

I could place some of Mike's ashes in Megan's coffin and she agreed. It was too surreal. I was numb as I witnessed the pain on the faces of her family and friends and again with Mike's friends. They looked shocked and amazed as they kept shaking their heads saying, "They're together again." I tenderly placed a red, heart shaped pillbox with Mike's ashes near Megan's heart. Helen was still there by my side and let me know when it was time to leave.

The next day we met Ed and some of Mike's friends at the church for the funeral. Pete drove in from Knoxville for the service. He, too, was in a state of disbelief. Patty had asked if I would like to speak at the service, along with Megan's aunt and cousin. I felt honored to be asked and wanted to do that for Megan and her family. I said a few words about Megan and how much our friendship had developed since Mike's death. As I announced the name of the poem I was to read, gasps were heard throughout the church. The poem was *When Tomorrow Starts Without Me.*

The burial was difficult; she was buried two plots away from Mike. Ed, Pete and I stood at Mike's grave holding hands along with Mike's friends. It was too unbelievable, too bizarre, too hard to grasp. No one really knew how to express their feelings. Mike and Megan were together, but not the way any of us ever envisioned.

We arrived at Megan's house for a few minutes after the service. When I handed Patty a copy of the poem, she told me her mother, Megan's grandmother, had given her the poem *When Tomorrow Starts Without Me* to read at her funeral. Maybe Megan guided me to the poem that day. Maybe that's why there were so many gasps at the funeral, but I also think it was too hard to hear those words – to final, too real, too much. But I knew that it was the way life would now be for Megan's family and friends.

A few days later I left for New Orleans. Helen took me to the airport and would not let me lift a suitcase. Helen, my seventy-year-old friend, with arthritis, was still taking care of me. She knew I wasn't supposed to be lifting or going out of town for that matter, but I needed to be with my family. I stayed at my bother Chip's house, with my niece Katie and her two-year-old son Dominic. They all made me feel comfortable and cared for. Katie was observant and wasn't afraid to talk to me about my grief and sorrow. She noticed my sadness and heartache and she tried to comfort me as I lay in bed one evening. Katie talked to me about Mike and Megan and she listened as I wept through reliving my memories. I spent a lot of time with T, Pete and Patrice, but I also found myself in bed resting much of the time. The fatigue and emotions had done a job on me. I wasn't much fun and I didn't feel much like celebrating. Things were too different now.

Pete stayed with me until Christmas morning, when he left to spend time with his dad's side of the family. His dad's birthday was also the day after Christmas and the family had a football game on Christmas day and a golf tournament on the following day. Ed's family knew how to celebrate everything New Orleans style, and I think Pete felt an escape with them. Most of the cousins were some of his greatest supporters in the next few years, especially when Pete left for his motorcycle trip to Mexico and Central America.

Chip's home had now become the setting for Christmas dinner and he was the host. It was an uncommonly cold day for New Orleans as my family gathered there for the afternoon dinner and celebration. I felt as if I was on the outside looking in, so detached from the holiday joy, and excused myself for a long nap. I awoke to the sounds of excitement in the air. I rose to see what all the chatter was about and found that it was actually snowing in New Orleans! My family was out with Dominic laughing and playing in the snow. I watched from the doorway, too cold and weak to join in the playfulness. If I had only remembered then what Mike had told me in a dream – that I would know his presence through glitter, the wind and snowflakes – I would have been out there, no matter how I felt. But maybe the gift was simply observing my family playing with Dominic for his first experience in the snow. I had always felt Dominic knew Mike on the Other Side before he was born, just a few weeks after Mike left us. How special now when I look back and see the gift. Mike gave me that gift through the joy of seeing Dominic enjoying and playing in the snowflakes. I know Mike was with me and helping me experience the joy through the sorrow and the tears as I watched Dominic build his snowman. I'd like to believe both Mike and Megan were there, enjoying the snow with him.

It was a celebration of life in this world that Mike wanted me to acknowledge until I was with him on the Other Side.

When Tomorrow Starts Without Me

When tomorrow starts without me and I'm not there to see,
If the sun should rise and find your eyes all filled with tears
for me.
I wish so much you wouldn't cry the way you did today,
While thinking of the many things we didn't get to say.
I know how much you love me, as much as I love you.
And each time you think of me, I know you'll miss me too.

But when tomorrow starts without me, please try to
understand
That an angel came and called my name and took me by
the hand
And said my place was ready in Heaven far above,
And that I'd have to leave behind all those I dearly love.
But as I turned and walked away, a tear fell from my eye,
For all my life I'd always thought I didn't want to die.

I had so much to live for and so much yet to do,
It seemed almost impossible that I was leaving you.
I thought of all the yesterdays, the good times and the bad.
I thought of all the love we shared and all the fun we had.
If I could relive yesterday, I thought just for a while,
I'd say goodbye and kiss you and maybe make you smile.

But then I fully realized that this could never be,
For emptiness and memories would take the place of me.
And when I thought of worldly things that I'd miss come
tomorrow,
I thought of you, and when I did, my heart was filled with
sorrow.

163

But when I walked through Heaven's gates, I felt so much at home,
When God looked down and smiled at me from His great golden throne.

He said, "This is eternity and all I've promised you.
Today your life on earth is past but here it starts anew."
So when tomorrow starts without me, don't think we're far apart
For every time you think of me, I'm right here in your heart.

- Author unknown

Pete's Journey to Healing

I worried about Pete finding some peace and healing as he dealt with his own pain of Mike leaving him so early. They had made plans for the future and even talked about their kids growing up with each other. Pete never found an outlet for his grief and anger and loss, although he tried often. Then, in the spring of 2006, he called to tell me he had bought a used motorcycle. I didn't know where this idea came from, but I did know his neighbor, Mike (yes, another Mike), was into motorcycles and I was excited to hear something was finally sparking his interest.

Pete rode his new motorcycle determinedly to get accustomed to the road with only two wheels under him and to learn the ins and outs of the unspoken "motorcycle code." I later realized it was really just practice for what was to come. Pete was very much the adventurer. He also learned quickly; his teachers used to say he was like a sponge. A few months later Pete told me he had "graduated" to a bigger bike – a BMW 650 road bike and he and his buddy Mike intended to take a road trip. I felt it would be a good outlet for Pete, as long as they weren't planning to go to Mexico or South America. Well, so much for that thought.

Originally the trip was planned for Canada, then Pete broke the news – they were going to cross the country from Knoxville to California, then head for Mexico and Central America, and if time permitted, continue throughout South America. My heart dropped. "Why Mexico and Central America?" I asked, knowing how bad things were in those poverty-stricken countries and realizing the dangers and hardships they would face. But I couldn't oppose Pete's answer. "Mom, Mike (his brother) changed everything." I couldn't argue with that. My only response was for him to go, I loved him, but be careful and take care of himself. Pete met with a lot of controversy over his decision from much of my family and his dad's family. But I knew he had to do what was his to do. It was very much like my trip to Carolina Beach when I checked out from reality. This was Pete's journey to "check out" from reality, and hopefully find serenity and some kind of acceptance.

I went to Knoxville to attend the going away party for Pete and his friend Mike. It was a hoot! So many of their friends were there wishing them well, yet none understood the true purpose of this trip for Pete. I accompanied Pete on his shopping excursions to get the equipment for the journey and to take care of financial details. I saw them off on December 6, 2006 and anxiously awaited the e-mails and phone calls I hoped to receive. I worried and I prayed;

166

yet I empathized. All Pete had to say was, "Mike changed everything."

I imagined the worst that could happen but prayed for the best. I wanted Pete to find his peace even if it meant my peace was totally unnerved. I remember hugging him and saying, "Go with God." I'm sure it was strange for Pete to hear those words from me. But he was on a mission. Mike had now sent *him* on a mission, and I most definitely was aware of Mike's *missions*. I could not stand in Pete's way, but only encourage him, let him know I loved him and wished him a fun, but meaningful and spiritual experience.

It's hard to explain, but I felt as long as Pete didn't encounter the Mexican jail system, I could handle the rest. If for some reason he didn't make it back safely, then it would be a sign that I could go. I could be with both of my boys. Don't get me wrong, I wanted Pete to find the release he had been searching for so long, but I had found a way to rationalize the concept of something happening to him. That was the only way I could deal with it – one way or the other – either Pete came out of the experience with peace and acceptance, having found his way, or we would all be together on the Other Side.

Again, don't misunderstand me. I was anxious to live for Pete and to be a big part of his life experience. I wanted to witness the expectations I had for Pete. He is so interesting, fun to be with, hard working and has a great sense of humor. When Pete is with you, he is with you. My joy consists of his visits to see me and my visits to see him. I know I would have given up on life if he were not a part of it. Pete was my mission, to be with him, to listen and to participate in his life as much as he would allow.

And now it was to follow as much of his trip as I could. His passion for this adventure was amazing to witness, as well as infectious.

For almost five months my days were filled with the expectations of Pete's phone calls and e-mails. They were frequent during most of the cross-country trip, before he crossed the border into Baja. Then they stopped. Pete was out of cell-phone reach and the cord was severed. Now I had to rely on the few one or two-minute phone calls and the e-mails he was able to send when he found a place with phone and e-mail access. The e-mails were very clever and funny, but I always knew when he wasn't telling me something. For example, he nonchalantly e-mailed, "We're holding up here for a few days." When he got home I found out those "few days" were because he had a pretty bad accident and needed the time to heal.

Pete and Mike met up with two other guys doing the same trip, Tom from London and Mavy from Australia. They became one team on a similar journey. He told me of the times he and his buddies had to take ferries, which were really only large rowboats, to avoid the bandito roads. He told me of the repeated times people told him the "angels were with all of them." He told me of the times when people took them in and fed them and helped them along their way. Usually those in the most need themselves, were the ones to help the guys. He told me about the family who invited them to their daughter's sixteenth birthday party. Pete told me he had never witnessed so much poverty. He told me about riding through a field of bulls and being "a little worried" because he had a red bike. It was the big things he didn't tell me until he returned home. For example, one bull was chasing him so close, Pete could hear him breathing. He told me about the fearful ride down a mountain, with such massive winds, that the bikes were actually sideways as they rode and witnessed the bus and truck graveyard below. He told me about the scary and terrifying ride he and Mike took over a train trestle, with no sides, and the raging river below, in order to make it home in time for Mike's game. There were no roads at that point. I'm glad I didn't know the reality of these experiences while he was on his journey. Pete and "his team" were just living day-to-day, and really minute-to-minute, never knowing what was around the bend. They encountered so many experiences and characters along their journey, some good and some not so good. They experienced breakdowns, wrecks, escapes from the banditos, being robbed, sleeping in the jungle, sleeping on the beach and having fish tacos for breakfast, climbing a volcano from the wrong side of the mountain and having to slash their way through the dense jungle for hours, but I do believe the wonder of it all far outweighed the trials.

Pete's experiences on his journey are his to tell, but he did acknowledge there was not a moment he didn't feel Mike was with him and now he felt Mike was a part of him. After hearing all the trials and tribulations of his trip I understood that statement.

Pete's trip helped me in more ways than I could ever explain. I lived vicariously through him and knew we were still here for a reason. When he returned to Charlotte the Saturday afternoon before Mike's annual softball game, I could see the difference in him. I could see the calm composure and the transformation of my son. Something happened to him on that trip which only Pete can express, but it was there for all to see and recognize. Several people at the game the next day didn't even recognize him. He came home thinner, with long hair and a beard. He's still that nonconformist person today. The autonomy Pete experienced on his journey seemed to agree with him.

I can only feel that Mike has touched both of us in a way we can never question or take for granted. We both know in our hearts and souls Mike is right here, right next to us, guiding us on our way and encouraging us to continue with this life until we are all together again.

Today and Tomorrow

It's been more than seven years since Mike left and I'm still trying to find that "new normal." I started to recognize a difference sometime after the fifth year as I began going out to lunch with friends and even on a beach trip with the Woo Woos again. The beach trip used to be an annual trip we enjoyed to the Carolina coast (there's that "used to be"). I felt I had come so far, and I had, but Helen recently told me I'm still hiding out. Maybe there's some truth to that. It's my old enthusiasm and joy I'm still searching to find. Oh, I can put on a good face at work and when I'm out with friends, but it's not the same. I usually can't wait to get home to my cave. Lately I've attributed some of the depression to the "empty nest syndrome" – both my sons are gone in one way or another. Pete's been in Knoxville since 1996 and he has a very busy and interesting life there. His visits home aren't as frequent since he has to split visits between Charlotte and New Orleans (where his dad and our family reside).

I get very excited and I feel my old enthusiasm when I visit Pete. His "family of friends" live in Knoxville. They are all from different places and stayed in the city after school. He recently bought a ninety-three-year old home in a foreclosure, which he renovated himself, so he's not been to Charlotte as much as the years before. He has a lot on his plate with work and renovations. I visited several times during the yearlong house restoration, and I enjoyed every minute with him – painting, scraping walls and cleaning up the dirt and sawdust. This past Labor Day weekend he sent out a text message to Mike's friends explaining he needed a truck and a helper to rebuild Mike's arbor over my patio – it became twisted in a windstorm. That weekend we had five of Mike's friends building a new arbor with Pete. It was a wonderful weekend, as I enjoyed seeing the guys working so hard on that bright autumn day, working to make Mike's arbor a beautiful gift once more. My boys were, and still are, my life, as are their "family of friends."

It's still hard to relate to some people when speaking about Mike. When I talk about him I feel the shut down from others, mostly from the ones who never knew Mike. It makes them uncomfortable because they don't really know what to say or how to react when I talk about him. I wish they could just accept that I had two sons and realize I need to speak about him, just as they speak about their own children. But, I realize over time that is often too much to ask. I feel as though I have to be cautious when speaking to those who didn't know me or Mike or Pete as we were as a family. They just don't understand. Mike is as much a part of my life now as he ever was before he crossed over.

Mike's room is still basically the same. I have my desk and computer in his bedroom now and I often spray a little Nautica cologne while I'm working. I need that scent around his room to help keep him close to me.

There are many additions to his room. The striking and touching portrait of Mike my niece, Katie, painted from Mike's high school photograph that first year, and lovingly framed by Megan, now hangs above the head of his bed. Megan made sure she delivered the painting when Pete was in town, so we could both enjoy and appreciate the beautiful gift. On another wall I've hung the poignant collage Megan created after Mike's death. It depicts Mike's baseball career during high school. The photos show him in different stances – receiving the pitch, hitting the ball and running to first base. In the middle of the color photos is a black and white photo of Mike looking back over his shoulder with that look he had when he looked into your heart and soul. It almost looks as if he's saying good-bye. It's hard sometimes to behold, but other times, it brings a joy to my heart as I remember watching all his games, and remembering how athletically talented he was. And then there's the awe-inspiring collage Amanda assembled for her design class, in memory of Mike, which included depictions of a fishing pole, the horse Mike was supposed to ride, the label of gin he liked, the Marlboro Lights he smoked, and several photos of butterflies and angels, along with his last photograph from our Pensacola brunch. It's so Mike. Those two collages lovingly depict the essence of Mike very well. On his dresser sits a statue of a baseball player, with the nameplates "Lovebug" on one side and "Big Worm" on the other, from Chip, T, and Katie in honor of his birthday and "The Game." Yes, it's a Mikie shrine. I also have a Mikie shrine on a shelf in my curio cabinet. Pete has one too.

Many of the significant symbols of Mike I experienced through my eyes, after his death, are illustrated in a stunning and very meaningful painting that T had commissioned for me to commemorate Mike's sixth anniversary. It includes a double rainbow and a hawk soaring in the clear, blue sky carrying a worm in its beak. She did think of everything.

There are two stars named for Mike. One, which I found very touching, is from Serena, and the star deed reads "Michael Ludman." The other is from T, which reads "Lovebug." Now when I gaze upon the heavens, I search for Mike's twinkling star light, knowing he is still a guiding light to us all.

Things are different from the first three or four years after Mike transitioned to the "Other Side." I can now talk about Mike without sobbing or going off in a daze of depression and sadness. I seldom cry as I'm driving anymore, unless something just totally blindsides me. The eerie fog lifted several years ago. But, as I've written about Mike, the longing for his presence returns. I miss him so much. I sometimes still retreat from my prior self in many ways. I think I'm progressing, but others often see me in another light. I'm still that "used to be." There is no getting over it and I know I'll never again be the person I used to be. But, I am no longer the shell of a person I had become. They say everything that happens to us makes us stronger, and the person we are meant to be. I've heard too often, "Why me?" and then I think, "Why not me?"

A while ago, a friend sent me a card, which states, "What if all the things that seem so unfair turn out to make sense after all? What if every life drama we needed for the growth of our soul was provided for us?" That card was very hard to accept at the time, but it hangs on my bathroom mirror as a reminder each day. After all, this journey in life is really like school, a learning experience we need to joyfully reach the "Other Side."

I'm writing again and look forward to fulfilling those dreams. Mike told me in a letter once, "Never give up on your dreams, Mom, or you've lost them." I don't intend to disappoint him. I already have the first paragraph in my head for my next book – it will be fiction. This book was way too hard for me, yet healing.

I feel as if the things I liked to do previously, and the friendships I enjoyed are still there for me. Old friends are appearing back in my life, people I never expected to even see or converse with again. It's strange. I've been very blessed with wonderful, caring friends and family, and I long to be a part of those things I once enjoyed in my life. I look forward to whitewater rafting trips, for as long as I can handle them physically. Pete and I enjoyed a rafting trip on the Ocoee River for my birthday this past August. It was probably one of the best trips I've ever had on whitewater. It appears that old adventurer in me is starting to surface again. I'm still anticipating my first zip lining experience, hopefully in the near future with other daring friends, old and young. I look forward to enjoying my grandchildren one day. I can't wait to send them home howling at the moon and spoiling them – one day.

I still have my life to live and I hope to do it joyously. I see myself, after retirement, living with T and friends in a large house with a rocking chair porch, somewhat like the *Golden Girls*. I think that will be a blast and a renewal of life for me. I've been told by more than one person that this book will open doors for a new life for me, and dealing with the pain will bring me to a new beginning. I am so looking forward to the new beginning – a new and fulfilling chapter in my life. Yes, Mike will always be a part of it, but I'll be living for him the way he intended me to live. I will live for Pete, for Mike and myself. I will be the person I was meant to be – living life again.

Come Sit with Me

You tell me that I'm different, that I am not who I used to be,
If you'll sit down here beside me, I will try to help you see.

You see God has changed my life forever when he took away my boy,
Now my heart is in so many pieces, and it's too hard to find any joy.

I know to you it's been a while and you say, you know it's been over a year,
But there is so much pain here deep inside me and so much sadness with every tear.

You say you know, I lost a parent or maybe an uncle, or even a friend,
And I know to you that pain is awful, but loosing a child will change you to the bitter end.

No, I'm not saying that I'm bitter, but sometimes I am angry and I guess even mad.
He was so young and just getting started; there was so much life he should have had.

For him there will never be a wedding or no new home for me to see,
Not one thing that I wished for him will ever happen or come to be.

So please be thankful for your children, enjoy the things
they say and do,
Even the days they make you angry, don't forget to say, "I
love you".

You see you never know if tomorrow will come for them, or
even you,
So don't just tell them that you love them, let them feel it in
all you do.

With God's help I know I'll make it, but you see I struggle
here every day,
As he molds me and he makes me, I know he's with me
along the way.

So now you know why I am different, and you're right, I'm
not who I used to be.
So thank you for sitting down here beside me and taking
the time to try to see.

By Lisa Roark

Through the Eyes of His Friends

"Your son was there for me when I needed a friend."

— Jessica

"He was a very loyal friend and teammate."

— Ryan

"Mike was such a beautiful person . . . I wanted to tell him how much I loved him and wanted to thank him for helping me succeed in life. Your son made such an impact on my life."

— Stacey

"He was a wonderful guy who I grew to love, respect and look up to! He made me laugh every time I saw him."

— Libby

"We all loved Mike. He put a smile on all our faces."
— Breena

"He took really good care of his friends."
— Amanda

"When you walked into a room and Mike was there, you knew right away — you could feel his presence."
— Kelly

"The first time I met Mike I was in junior high. I was really hanging out with Pete. Mike was dressed like it was 1967, yet I was drawn to him because he was Pete's brother. I would see Mike in the halls at school, and I had a feeling that he would be the icing on the cake if he were to become a part of the new crew that formed. It didn't take long for his appearance to change. He hung up the Birkenstocks and the tie-dyes and started to look more like the rest of the guys. Finally, we made it to the Big East (high school). We wore baggy clothes, grew some cool beards, and were under the influence of hip-hop. The only reason we got respect was because Mike was Pete's younger brother. Back to Mike being the icing on the cake, he was the leader of the pack."
— (From the short story titled,
Boys Will Be Boys)
— Sean

"Mike was a very caring person. He always put his friends first (well family, then friends) before anything. He would give you his last dollar if you needed it or, in my case, his last shoe. He was like one of us, a Weethee, and that's why we clicked so much. When I would come over Mike would

be upstairs listening to music. I'd knock on the door and he would come downstairs with a big smile on his face, as if he was about to say or do something totally childish. Just a big kid! When you needed a laugh, he was the one that would have you cracking up! Mike had a great sense of humor. We were all brothers and we would sit around and talk about anything and everything. We just enjoyed each others' company. I still see Mike in a lot of us when we are all together, but I just can't touch him . . . I wish I could. I would put my arm around him and just say, ' Thanks, man' and smile. Because of him, we are all family. Man, I miss him!"

– Lou

"One of the main things about Mike was his generosity and the respect he received. Mike was always looking out for all of us. If he was looking for a wing man to hang with, whether it was just to have a beer or run errands, he would take care of you. None of us had any money, but Mike was always generous with whatever he had. If it was a beer or a smoke, you had a beer or a smoke. He took me golfing one time when I didn't have any money to play, just because he wanted to go and wanted me to come too. He would also look out for the girlfriends too. I remember several times he would go into a gas station and, not only check if I wanted anything, but would also ask if my girl wanted anything too. If you tried to give him any money, he would get insulted and look at you like you were crazy. I think he truly enjoyed taking care of his friends.

Mike was also trying to hook us up and play matchmaker with Megan's friends. It really didn't benefit him to do that,

181

but I think it made him happy to hook up the fellas. Most people you have to ask, 'Hey man, does your girl have any friends?' With Mike, he was already looking for girls for you. Basically, Mike would do anything he could to make sure his friends were taken care of. It made him happy to make sure you were happy.

Also, when I think of him, I remember his serious, yet playful demeanor. He reminded me of a little kid trapped in a grown man's body. He could be so goofy and silly at times. It was funny because his goofy side was totally opposite of people's perception of him. Those who didn't really know him at school thought he was this mean looking dude who was not to be 'messed with'. He wasn't to be 'messed with' for sure, but it was funny to think that if those people really knew him, they'd have known this guy was a big teddy bear. That's the kind of respect Mike always got from everyone, all of us included. He was not only loved by all different types of people, but was also respected as well. Mike commanded respect, but it was always given to him without question. Many of us have polarizing personalities – you love us or you hate us. Not Mike – everyone loved him. I don't think I've come across anyone else in my life that was as respected by so many people as was Mike. He was truly deserving of the respect he received.

Sometimes, he reminded me of the Godfather, not in a bad way, just the way that people looked up to him and respected him. It's the reason, year after year, so many people come out to the game to pay their respect to him. He was truly one of a kind."

– Nelson

On August 17, 2002 I was sitting at the top of a mountain in Vail, Colorado with my little brother, Sean. As I sat there looking out over God's beautiful creation, I felt the wind leave my chest. I gasped for air, knowing something had happened, I just didn't realize at the time what it was. After returning to Charlotte, I received a phone call from my Mom. As soon as I heard her voice I knew she was calling with bad news. "Megan Miles just came to see me and I have some really terrible news to tell you. Megan, Mike died in a car accident yesterday. I'm so, so sorry!" The words stung me like a knife, cutting directly thru my chest. I literally dropped the phone, I couldn't move. I knew at that moment what it was I had felt on that mountaintop in Vail; my dear, sweet, precious friend left this world!! It was the last thing on earth I ever wanted to hear.

Mike Ludman was a dear friend to me at a time when I needed him so much. After a very difficult relationship with an ex who abused me both physically and mentally, I had gotten into a lot of trouble and was facing very serious felony charges. Mike was there for me during a time when I had given up on any hope in life. I had lied to family and friends, hurt the people that had loved me the most and had betrayed their trust. The friend I had in Mike was the kind of love and support that got me through one of the most difficult times of my life.

He was my angel during his short time on earth and I know he's now a true angel watching over all of us. Giving us those feelings sometimes, when we just know he's right there with us. Mike always used to tell me, "Smile that beautiful smile Megan, because there is happiness ahead." Somehow he knew and his reassurance, kindness, and support were the exact things I needed to give me the strength to make it through one of my life's most difficult trials. We all have them, and I was blessed to have Mike in my corner when I needed him the most. He made me laugh, when all I wanted to do was cry. He was the one who first introduced me to Remy VSOP so we could have a few drinks and forget our troubles for a while and the one who indulged my love for "Pretty Woman," watching it with me on more than one occasion.

We were very close through my court problems, but after some time passed, situations changed and we had not seen each other in a while before he died. One of my deepest regrets, is that I hadn't heard his voice in several months, and when I heard he was gone I knew I wouldn't hear it again, at least not in this life. This world was a better place for him having been in it. His smile lit up the lives of so many and his memory will always live on in the ones that were lucky enough to have known him.

I am so blessed and thankful to be one of those people. Mike made me believe in life when I wanted to give up on it, and when I found out he was gone, I wanted to be mad at God, and I was, for a while. But because death is something that has always been a part of my life and I know we are always at risk of losing those closest to us, I choose to look to the light, like my dear friend Mike always told me. I got over my anger and tried to remember the good times. I have a loving husband and three wonderful stepsons and I never take a day for granted. Mike Ludman was a dear friend whom I will miss always and I will always be grateful for the person he was to me. MISS YOU & LOVE YOU ALWAYS MIKIE!

– Megan (Mike's friend)

And If I Go

And if I go,
While you're still here …
Know that I live on,
Vibrating to a different measure —
Behind a veil you cannot see through.
You will not see me,
So you must have faith.
I wait for the time when we can soar together again —
Each fully aware of the other.
Until then, live your life to its fullest and when you need
me,
Just whisper my name in your heart
… I will be there.

Author unknown

Contact information for those who contributed their time and talent:

Author: Diane Ludman
DML23@carolina.rr.com

Editor: Joanna Sheldon
joannaleighsheldon@yahoo.com

Cover Design: Cindy Gaines Nims
cindygaines1080@yahoo.com

Poetry: Lisa Roark
momld@bellsouth.net

Psychic-Medium: Mary Beth Wrenn
marybethwrenn@yahoo.com

KinderMourn: Kelly Hamilton, Director
Elizabeth Pearce, Counselor/Facilitator
www.kindermourn.org
    704-376-2580

Made in the USA
Columbia, SC
13 September 2024

42196790R00113